Of Life and Love

Of Life and Love

James P. Lisante

Foreword by

John Powell, S.J.

Revised Edition

Resurrection Press
Mineola, New York

Original edition published in 1989 by

    Resurrection Press, Ltd.
    P.O. Box 248
    Williston Park, NY 11596
Revised edition published in 1991.

ISBN 1-878718-06-1
Library of Congress Catalog Number 91-60258

Cover by Meg C. Bennett and John Murello

Photo credits: Thomas F. Moloney
                 The Long Island Catholic

Printed in the United States of America by Faith Printing.

Dedication

To my nephews Jonathan, Matthew Paul, and Anthony, and my niece Marisa, whose lives fill me with hope. You are my inspiration and I carry you, forever, in my heart and soul.

Acknowledgements

Many good people shared in the publication of this book, and I wish to offer them my deepest thanks.

They include my wonderful parents, Cecelia and Nicholas Lisante; my sisters, Patti and Joan; my publisher, Dr. Nancy Benvenga; my editor at *The Long Island Catholic*, Monsignor Francis J. Maniscalco; my assistant, Julietta Rosst; and Patricia Flynn, office manager at the Family Ministry apostolate.

Special thanks, too, go to Bishop John R. McGann for his enormous dedication to the cause of Family Life and Respect for Life programs in the Diocese of Rockville Centre, New York.

Finally, I am grateful to Father John Powell, S.J. and Archbishop Roger Mahony for their encouragement and friendship.

Father Jim Lisante
May 1989

Contents

Preface by *Rev. Archbishop Roger Mahony*

Foreword *by Fr. John Powell, SJ*

1.	A Courageous Woman	1
2	The Pro-Life Vision of Frank Capra	4
3.	Sex Respect	6
4.	"Boom, Boom, Boom"	8
5.	Pornography: We All Lose	10
6.	On Fear and Love	12
7.	Sinners and Saints	14
8.	January 22nd	16
9.	Show the Pictures	18
10.	"Don't Worry, Be Happy"	20
11.	When It Just Hurts Too Much	23
12.	Life Gives Hope	25
13.	Coming Clean	28
14.	Parents	30
15.	Mothers	32
16.	No Sacrifice At All	35
17.	Can We Talk?	37
18.	On Being Catholic and Proud	39
19.	We Are Not Alone	41
20.	Champions of Life	44
21.	Interfaith Marriage	46
22.	Self-Esteem	50
23.	Being Consistent	52
24.	A Family Perspective	54
25.	Family Perspective II	57

26. Good Friends 60

27. Getting Off the Ride 62

28. Remembering Michael 64

29. Going to Church 66

30. Our Inconvenient Savior 68

31. On Being "Perfect" 70

32. Father Gerry and Susan 72

33. Foolish Feminism 74

34. Seamless Garment: Dirty Words? 76

35. What We Really Believe 78

36. Parental Consent 80

37. School-Based Health Clinics:
    No Answer At All 83

38. Informed Consent 85

39. All the News That Fits 87

40. Of Polls and Persons 90

Bishop John McGann of Rockville Centre, Father John Powell, S.J. and Father Jim Lisante at a Respect Life Prayer Meeting in Wantagh, N.Y.

Archbishop Roger Mahony of Los Angeles, staunch supporter of human rights and a leading figure in the Respect Life movement.

Preface

Every now and then there comes along a columnist who is able to combine personal experience, contemporary cultural and societal realities, common sense and a deep faith in Jesus Christ in a truly remarkable fashion. Father James Lisante is that columnist in our own time, and all of us across the country are both grateful and proud of his sound pro-life and pro-family writings.

I am delighted that a set of his columns is being published under the title *Of Life and Love,* and therefore, made available to a wider audience.

Father Jim Lisante has the extraordinary ability to identify with clarity and concern current trends in our society, most of which are shallow and short-lived. Father Jim brings depth and commitment to the great gift of God's life towards us. He models in beautiful language that love which we must share as disciples and followers of our Lord Jesus Christ.

Father Jim's total dedication to the Respect Life movement, together with his ability to speak to all age groups and audiences, make him a national grace for our entire Church. May this book of essays fall into the hands of our young people who are searching for God and meaning in their lives, as well as all Catholics and Christians who value the unique design and plan for human life given to all of us by God our Creator.

Archbishop Roger Mahony
Los Angeles, California

Foreword

For a long time psychologists have been looking at and studying the troubled and sick. They wonder, "How did you get so sick?" But more recently there has arisen a new approach in the field that looks for well people, and asks, "How did you ever get so well?"

Are you, perhaps, like me? I find myself looking for (and often finding) Christian heroes. I somehow need to see the health and happiness of Christianity incarnated in someone. I mean someone who laughs and loves and prays. To paraphrase G.K. Chesterton: "Christianity hasn't really failed. It is just that we haven't really tried it yet." Sure, we're only on our way home. We're not there yet. But I find myself looking along the path for "alleluia" people, people who know what it is to enjoy the trip.

In any case, I am always keeping my eye peeled and my ear perked for someone who obviously knows that the Gospel is "good news." I look for people who enjoy being who they are, but who can get beyond themselves and self-interest. I listen for the sounds of love and compassion in the voices of others. I watch for the sights of love as eagerly as we watch for the first sign of tulips in the springtime.

I have spent only one evening watching Father Jim Lisante. We had previously exchanged a few letters. But even these few letters were enough to arouse my curiosity. The man sounded so upbeat and positive. He sounded like a happy and gifted "good-finder." "He likes people. He looks beyond human frailty to uncover human goodness," I said to myself. Then I met the man. I listened to him speak. He gave off all the right signs and sounds. Since then, I have read his writing, and have come to realize that what we have here is a real Christian. He isn't off somewhere in the proverbial ivory tower. He doesn't have the dark cloud of doom hovering over his head. I secretly think of those people as having "spiritual bad breath." Jim Lisante, by contrast, is a breath of fresh air. I want to ask, "How did you ever get so well?"

His writing travels along the risky road of self-revelation. He talks about himself and his own collisions with reality. But it isn't the tiring narcissism of self-absorption. He laughs a lot, and he can laugh at himself. This is always a good sign. As the old Chinese beatitude has it: "Blessed are they who can laugh at themselves. They will never cease to be entertained."

Lastly, Father Jim Lisante is a man with a life-giving message. Someone has said, "Try to learn from the mistakes of others. You won't live long enough to make them all yourself." I like to read the words of someone who says between the lines, "I think I have learned this somewhere along my own way. Now I want to share my own process and journey with you. That way you won't have to make all the mistakes I've made. I want to share with you whatever I have learned so your own life journey and your personal process can profit from mine." This sentiment is very audible between all the lines you are about to read.

I am most happy to recommend this laughing and loving human being, who is fully human, fully alive, and fully Christian. What he has to say is well worth listening to and what he has written is well worth reading. He who is mighty has done some very fine things in this good man.

John Powell, S.J.
Loyola University
Chicago, Illinois
April 1989

A Courageous Woman

I remember vividly my first sight of Patricia Neal. My parents, back in 1968, took us to see a movie called *The Subject Was Roses*. I thought she was fantastic. My admiration for her deepened greatly when I learned that her performance in that film followed rehabilitation from a series of serious strokes. With determination and extraordinary courage she had battled the ravages of a body and mind that were badly impaired. She had "fought the good fight" and been unwilling to let her illness destroy her. She still had a lot of living to do! During her rehabilitation she was also carrying an unborn child. The experience of childbirth is a trauma for even those in the fittest of shapes. But for a woman coming out of three major strokes, the burden of giving birth was immense. People could (and probably did) argue that the pregnancy should be terminated. But that route was never a serious possibility for Patricia Neal. She'd been down that road before. She knew it was a dead end!

The strokes were not Pat's first experience in monumental family crisis. She had a beautiful daughter named Olivia who died of complications from measles. That death was overwhelming for Pat. She also suffered from the senseless tragedy of seeing her only son injured in a car accident in New York City. The child's nurse inadvertently pushed his baby carriage into the street, and a passing car sent the child flying. Theo was brain damaged by the impact, giving Pat yet another reason to empathize with the handicapped and the disabled.

Several years ago I asked this incredible woman to speak at a benefit for the handicapped. She came gladly and spoke to a packed house about the experiences of her life. And, somehow, the drama of her films seemed but a shadow of the real experiences of her life. As she left the stage I remember that the auditorium exploded. People stood and clapped and cried. They were in awe of the seeming indomitability of the human spirit.

There was, however, one tragedy about which Patricia Neal did not speak. It came up in conversation, but never in public. Back in the early 1950s Pat had an affair with a man she really loved. He was the actor Gary Cooper. By him she became pregnant. For a multitude of fearful and confused reasons they chose to

1

abort their child. Now, there are some notables who, when they've aborted, rationalize the experience, "It was really best for everyone," or, "I've never regretted my decision," or, "It was difficult but necessary." Pat never did that. She knew it was wrong to end life. And the clarity of what she chose to do has never been watered down or minimized. I had hoped, as I grew to know and treasure Pat as a friend, that one day she might share her experience with others. I sensed that it would be liberating for her and a true education for those who trivialize the awesome horror of abortion.

Thank God, she has.

In her autobiography *As I Am*, Miss Neal writes of her abortion with candor and regret. She names it as the worst mistake of her life, one she has lived to regret for many years. "For over thirty years, alone in the night, I cried. If I had only one thing to do over in my life, I would have that baby," she writes. Patricia Neal says that she wishes she'd had the courage to have that baby. And while she recognizes that having a baby out of wedlock in the early 1950s would have been scandalous, she also voices her admiration for Ingrid Bergman who faced worldwide condemnation for conceiving her child through an extramarital relationship but who chose to give life instead of taking it, regardless of the cost. Writes Neal, "I admired Ingrid Bergman for having her son. She had guts. I did not. And I regret it with all my heart."

Pat Neal went on to marry and have five other children. They are each precious to her. But there was a sixth child she misses dearly, whom she never had the chance to know. She has come forward now to let others know the pain and sorrow that accompanies the choice called abortion. Her sharing is yet another powerful witness to the continuous courage of this wonderful woman. Her forthrightness may cost her some friends in the "liberal" community. Many will be upset that she sees abortion for the tragedy that it is. But such displeasure won't upset this valiant soul.

A final story. One night, after a delightful dinner in New York City, I was driving Miss Neal back to the country home in which she was staying. She was speaking about some of the major crises of her life. As we sped along the parkway, another car came up fast behind us. The driver was obviously drunk or drugged, careening from side to side of the road at a dangerous speed. Sure enough, as he passed, his car smashed us on Patricia's side. The intoxicated driver rode on while we pulled to the side of the road. People stopped to see that we were all right. And aside from frayed nerves, we were. After a while we got back in our car to continue the journey home. Incredibly, Miss Neal picked up the storytelling at the precise sentence she'd been on at the impact! (Nothing throws this lady.)

A warm, caring, compassionate and intelligent giant of a

woman, Patricia Neal gives us all yet another lesson in the catechism of courage. Thank you, Patricia, for allowing us to share in the sorrow of your abortion. With your help, others may choose life.

The Pro-Life Vision
of Frank Capra

Each year at Christmas our televisions seemed packed with specials to celebrate the season. Beyond doubt, the most popular film during this holiday is a 1946 classic called *It's a Wonderful Life*. Directed by film-maker Frank Capra (now in his nineties), it stars Jimmy Stewart, Donna Reed and Lionel Barrymore.

The movie tells the story of a man named George Bailey. He is filled with dreams and hopes and possibilities in his youth. He wants to travel, to experience life fully, to be a success, to collect many possessions, to have a good time.

But throughout his life he has to make choices between what's selfish and what's selfless. And these choices mean that his dreams often evaporate. Because when you choose to walk through the door of goodness and giving, you also close other doors that might lead to personal pleasure. George chooses to live for others and sometimes the giving causes him to "burn out."

One night, on Christmas Eve, his spirits are particularly low. He contemplates suicide. He believes that death would be preferable to living for others. Enter Clarence, George's guardian angel. Clarence helps George to see the richness in living for others. He shows George what life (for others) would have been like, had he never been born. And through this experience George comes to see that a life lived with generosity, with compassion, and with selflessness, is not only a wonderful life, but the only life worth living.

When we watch this delightful film, it's easy to get into feeling good, feeling sentimental and missing the great power this movie has to challenge us. Pope John Paul II says that we are on this planet to be "signs of contradiction" to a world which rejects the values of Jesus.

George Bailey is that contradiction. He's a person who celebrates a family life. He's faithful to his wife. And she's clearly a partner who is his best friend. They see children as a blessing, not a burden. As a family, their feelings are expressed openly

4

and honestly, even the disagreements. The Baileys also pray; they're not afraid to openly express their reliance on God.

Not all the Baileys are perfect. Like every family, they have problems, but the problematic member is loved, not denied. Uncle Billy, for example, is clearly an eccentric, a kind but befuddled man. The Baileys never mistreat this confused relation. They attempt, through patience and love, to fill in where Uncle Billy is lacking. In all that the Baileys do they reflect a belief in the sacredness of human life. In many ways, this forties film is prophetic. It celebrates the life forces presently under siege. It affirms family, children, the poor, the elderly, the infirm and the outcasts of society.

Capra, as he aged, recognized that his favorite film stood in direct opposition to the values of our culture. And in explaining the vision of *It's a Wonderful Life*, he said:

"It was my kind of film for my kind of people. A film to tell the weary, the disheartened, and the disillusioned, the wino, the junkie, the prostitute, those behind prison walls and those behind iron curtains, that no man is a failure!

"To show those born slow of foot or slow of mind, those oldest sisters condemned to spinsterhood, and those oldest sons condemned to unschooled toil, that each man's life touches so many other lives. And that if he isn't around it would leave an awful hole.

"A film that said to the downtrodden, the pauper, 'Heads up, fella. No man is poor who has one friend. Three friends and you're filthy rich.'

"A film that expressed its love for the homeless and the loveless; for those whose cross is heavy and him whose touch is ashes; for the Magdalenes stoned by hypocrites and the afflicted Lazaruses with only dogs to lick their sores.

"I wanted to shout to the abandoned grandfathers staring vacantly in nursing homes, to the always-interviewed but seldom-adopted half-breed orphans, to the paupers who refuse to die while medical vultures wait to snatch their hearts and livers, and to those who take cobalt treatments and whistle — I wanted to shout, 'You are the salt of the earth, and *It's a Wonderful Life* is my memorial to you!' "

I had the opportunity recently to visit with Mr. Capra. He is "on the mend" after several serious strokes. But weak as he sometimes is, his love of life, his concern for the unborn and the born never ebbs. And he delights in the knowledge that, long after he's gone home to God, his film will continue to proclaim, with incredible clarity, that every single life is a limitless gift from God, and that ours is a wonderful life!

Sex Respect

A couple of years back *Sassy* magazine ran an article that, for the most part, could have been written by a bishop. It's called "Virgins Are Cool," and it makes a strong case for saving sex for marriage. That's a big deal when you consider that *Sassy* is a new, with-it, trendy and popular secular publication for teenagers.

The Church often takes a bad rap about sex. People believe that Catholics see sex as dirty, as wrong, as sinful. We don't. We believe sex is beautiful, good and even holy. It's just a question of where you share it and what your motive is for giving one of the deepest parts of yourself to another person. The place to do it is in marriage. The reason to do it is real love.

For many years experts — psychologists and sociologists — have been grappling with the question: why do teenagers and young adults want sex? The obvious answer is that sex feels good. But that's way off the mark. There are, experts say, many non-sexual motives for why we desire sex. And coming to terms with why we want something can give us the courage to choose a better way of living.

In every report and study I've seen, these are the main reasons why we chase sex:

1. **Self-esteem**. We lack it. We want it. And we mistakenly believe that if we have sex we'll feel better about ourselves. Our teenage and young adult years can be filled with insecurity, confusion and sometimes emotional chaos. We'll grab at anything that promises to make us like ourselves better. The catch is sex won't do much to enhance our self-esteem, and probably will damage it — because self-esteem isn't based only on what we do (e.g., sex), but on who we are.

2. **Peer pressure**. None of us wants to be left out. If everybody is doing it, it's natural to want to join the crowd. The "crowd" is smaller than we think. Polling information confirms that about 32 percent of teenagers have sex before they graduate. That's bad news, but it sure doesn't represent a majority. In *Sassy*, author Karen Catchpole writes that people who don't have sex may think they are "weird, defective, undersexed...not cool."

Well, if that's what virgins are, then there are a lot of us there. Be relieved, we're not alone.

3. **I need love**. The culture in which we live has made some terrible equations. They've tried to convince us that sex equals love. It doesn't. In fact, in test studies of that 32 percent who have had sex, their response to the experience placed "love" way down the list of feelings they had after sex. Above it were "foolish," "used," "manipulated," "bad" and "regretful." And anyone who says that we prove our love by having sex is snowing you. Love doesn't have to be "proved." Love is a free gift, not one we have to pressure another into putting out.

4. **Rebellion**. From day one most of us have to answer to people in charge. Parents, teachers, coaches, older brothers and sisters, the Church, the principal. For many years we kind of accept the authorities who run our lives. But, inevitably, it happens. We decide to blow away the people in charge. One of the ways we do that is by rejecting their values and their rules. We stop going to Church. We try drinking and sometimes even drugs. We experiment with sex. These are ways in which we assert our independence. Don't mistake any of these actions for maturity or responsible freedom. They're adolescent responses to perceived frustrations. They're inappropriate reactions. The way we should respond to a need for greater freedom is to negotiate and reason with the authorities in our lives.

5. **Escape**. Our homes are not like Bill Cosby's. We don't have it all together. Conflict, division and unhappiness reign in many homes. People pick and nag. Celebrating the negative is how many parents respond to pressure. Young persons often crave escape from unhappy homes. One escape hatch that can promise temporary relief is sex. For just a few hours, at least, we think we can escape the hostile world we live in. But like most artificial escapes, the sexual release just puts us back where we started.

When I was a junior in high school my dearest friend died of cancer. She was a classmate and a tremendous person. For months after her death I did some incredibly stupid things, things I'd rather forget. Finally, after many mistakes, someone, at long last, confronted me: "Jim, don't you think you should deal with Chris' death instead of doing all these asinine things?"

That question hit me like a cold bucket of water in the face. I was avoiding the "why" of my behavior. And unless we know the why, we can never get out from under.

That's true of sex, too. We've got lots of motives for why we do what we do. And understanding our motives can give us the freedom to chose a better way.

"Boom, Boom, Boom"

Driving out east one Sunday morning I listened to the top 40 songs of the week. When we got to the superhits, the top five, I heard the words of a song which certainly deserved an award for directness. The refrain went like this:

"Boom, boom, boom, let's go back to my room, where we can do it all night, and you can make me feel right."

I continued to listen, wondering if the guy singing the song would develop the relationship beyond "boom, boom." He doesn't. And, sadly, neither do most guys.

In my work at the Family Ministry Office I get calls each week from teenage girls who find themselves in crisis pregnancy situations. They call looking for support and understanding. I always try to see them right away because I know that the pressure on them to "get rid of it" is enormous. And I always invite them to bring along their boyfriend, the father of the child. In almost eight out of ten cases the young woman shows up alone or with a girlfriend; sometimes with her mother or sister. When I ask her where her boyfriend is, the response is often, "He doesn't want to be involved," or "He wants me to get rid of it," or "He said he'd give me money for an abortion," or "He said, how do I know it's his?"

What we're dealing with here is what I call the "wimp factor." Guys, filled with macho braggadocio, talk a good game to assure their girlfriends of their undying love before and during a sexual touchdown. But bring a child into the picture, and you're more than likely going to see the tail end of their horses.

Teenage sexual activity almost necessarily lacks a sense of responsibility and of a permanent commitment to the other person. For the sexually active teen male, the tendency to cut and run when crisis challenges us to stick around and face the problem is nothing less than an admission of one's emotional inadequacy. Somewhere between "boom, boom" and a baby there's got to be a sense of owning what I do, accepting the consequences of my choices.

If you had the chance to catch the television program *Daddy*, you know what I mean. This drama, although flawed in parts, gave us a good sense of the connection between sex and the creation of new life. One very often leads to the other. And more importantly, it helped us to see that pregnancy is not just a woman's responsibility. Two people make love. Two people create a baby, and two people should accept the responsibility for the new and innocent life.

So before I decide (or let my body decide for me) to share myself completely with another human being, I've got to be real sure that I can live with the results of that sexual encounter. One of the best ways to check out the rightness or wrongness of what we do with our bodies is to ask ourselves some questions: Can I seriously see myself spending a lifetime with this particular person with whom I'm about to become involved? Could I ever really imagine being married to this presently attractive person? Can I begin to see myself as a Dad or a Mom? Do we have the financial means to support a child? Can I handle the mental and social stress of being a parent at my age? Would I be able to handle telling my parents that I'm pregnant or that I've helped someone to become pregnant? Putting it directly: Can I live with the consequences of sex beyond the "feel good" part of it? If my answer to these questions is no, then I'm probably also discovering the answer to the question of my readiness for sex right now. And so to anyone offering the experience of "boom, boom," the smart teenager will say, "Thanks, but no thanks."

Pornography: We All Lose

Before I was ordained, I worked for several years as a director of religious education in an urban parish. Part of the job, owing to my status as the only man on the school staff, was to spend time with the more "difficult" young people. I remember one student in particular, a boy named Charlie. He was in the eighth grade of the parish school and had been caught in class with some of the raunchiest pornography you can imagine. He was "sharing" it with his classmates and was mildly stunned when his teacher seized the goods! Charlie and I went for a walk. I purposely tried to relate in a relaxed way with him. I talked as if I found the porno as interesting as he did. And after befriending him, I mentioned that I knew people who dealt in these kinds of magazines and videos. Charlie was thrilled. To think that what he thought was going to be a strident lecture was turning into an opportunity to secure newer goods! And then, the conversation took a more surprising turn for our friend Charlie:

Charlie: "So you know where to get more of this stuff?"

Lisante: "Sure. I even know the people who publish it."

Charlie: "That's great!"

Lisante: "Yeah. In fact they're always looking for new people to put in their magazines. How would you feel about them putting a picture of your sister in, Charlie? Or your mother?"

Charlie: "That's really gross."

Yes, Charlie, it is. Only I wanted you to know that every person used by the pornography industry is a member of someone's family. In the midst of "enjoying" pornography, do we ever stop to think about that? Do we ever stop to consider how we would feel if we saw someone we love being used to tantalize? It's important to recognize that when we purchase or rent pornography, whether in magazines or videos or cable, we are paying people to dehumanize someone's daughter, someone's son, someone's sister, or someone's brother. We're reducing a human person to the level of an item we can buy. The person who appears in a pornographic enterprise becomes a "thingified" object, whose dignity is severely compromised.

Sometimes the feminist and pro-life movements seem locked in opposite directions. Our reaction to pornography, however, is

10

a source of unity. We all seem to acknowledge that this industry, which takes in some $8 billion a year in America alone, is a violation of the intent of the First Amendment of our Constitution. Clearly, our founding fathers never intended the word freedom to protect those who peddle flesh and degrade the personhood of people very much like us. Of particular concern is the "kiddie-porn" industry which continues to flourish in our nation. This vile destruction of the dignity of our young reduces the child/victim to a depravity unparalleled in modern times. And yet, amazingly, the American Civil Liberties Union sees even this abomination as a "protected and fundamental right."

To be truly pro-life involves a commitment to the whole person, from conception through natural death. Our fidelity to respect for life is made particularly manifest in our willingness to protect and defend the quality and dignity of all human life. Whenever a person is compromised through the pornography industry, we are all diminished. We are not just a piece of meat. We are a reflection of our Creator. Pornography mocks God in that it violates the beauty of his handiwork.

(For more information on what we can do to challenge the unlimited advantages of the pornography industry please write American Family Association, P.O. Drawer 2440, Tupelo, Miss. 38803 or phone 601-844-5036.)

On Fear and Love

A priest expects to visit the sick. It comes with the job, and is one of the reasons you become a priest to begin with. Like most of my brothers, I've visited many, many people affected with any number of infirmities. I'm not usually frightened when I visit a person who is ill, but one time I was terrified.

My friend Roseann called and asked me to visit her friend Adam. Sure, I replied, what hospital is he in? "He's not in a hospital," she replied. "He's beyond help." "What's the matter with him?" I asked. "He's dying of cancer, and he has AIDS," Roseann said. There was a long pause on the phone, and then, sensing my apprehension, she continued, "Are you afraid to go, Jim?" "No," I replied too quickly to be believed. "I'll be there on Friday."

The next few days were paralyzing. I've read as much as anyone about AIDS. I've even preached on it, naming it as a "great tragedy." But now I was going to meet the illness face to face. And, I'd be a liar if I didn't admit to absolute ignorance and prejudice. I looked for a dozen reasons to cancel my appointment with Adam. Surely I could find a way out. After all, what would I say to him, how would I relate to him and what about the risks? Whenever I visit a sick person I touch them. I hold their hands, I anoint them, and often I kiss them on the forehead. Surely, all those human touches were out of the question.

But, failing to find a good enough reason to cancel, I went to visit with Adam. All of my worst fears were realized quickly. He looked horrible, a skeleton of a man. His body was scarred with lesions, the apartment was still but smelled of illness. And, sure enough, I was no sooner in his presence, than he extended his weakened hand. Instinctively I grabbed it, flinching with ignorant fear inside. He coughed a bit, and I held my breath. Sensing my tenseness Adam asked me to sit and relax. I thanked him, sat and secretly wondered if the chair was contaminated. I gave in to all my fears, all my anxieties, all my ignorance. You don't catch AIDS from a chair, from a hand extended in welcome, from a cough. I knew all that in my head, but fear really screwed up good judgment. In a desperate attempt to make conversation and to channel my nervous energy, I got up to browse around the many photographs which lined the bedroom walls.

Adam had a lot of pictures. Pointing to what I thought might be his parents, I asked, "How are they dealing with all this?" "Not well," he answered. Then I came to another photo of a strikingly handsome young man, tan, in shape and with a blazing smile. "Your brother?" I asked. "No, Father Jim, that guy is me, last year." My heart sank, my eyes filled, and I blurted out, "I'm so sorry, Adam."

Something in that moment freed me. The life-altering pain and brokenness of this young man stilled my foolish fears. How could I, who carry a far lighter cross, allow there to exist any barrier of fear? I sat again and we talked and talked for hours. I held his hands without fear, I anointed him no more carefully than I would anyone else, and when I left, I kissed him gently on the forehead, grateful for the opportunity to have been with this courageous man who had accepted and cooperated with God's incomprehensible will.

I got back to my rectory and passed a bathroom on the first floor. Instinctively I moved to wash my hands, a reactive fear coming over me. But as I looked into the mirror I saw the greatest lesson of that visit with Adam. We are, all of us, like Adam. Human, frail, needful, dependent, sometimes beautiful, sometimes difficult to face, we are all, at times, difficult to love, to embrace, to accept. But, you know, if we can, with God's help, bring ourselves to kiss the Adams of this world, then we never need be afraid of anyone or anything again. Dear Adam, thank you for the lesson about living, and about dying, about fear and about freedom. May he rest in peace.

Sinners and Saints

Some months ago I had the privilege of interviewing a young football star named Mark Bavaro. He plays tight end for the New York Giants. People who know football well tell me that he's a truly outstanding player. All I know is that he's a man of enormous faith. And, as much as football means to Mark, he'll tell you without hesitation that God and his family are the most important values. At one point in our interview I asked Mark Bavaro how it felt to be a hero. Shortly before the program aired, Mark had met with a group of teenagers and young adults. Their eyes were fixed on this gentle giant. He really could do no wrong. Clearly, for them he was a hero.

In answer to my question, Bavaro debunked all the hero stuff. He doesn't believe we should make heroes of anyone in contemporary society, not athletes, not movie stars, not rock musicians, and not politicians. Our only true hero, he said, is Jesus Christ.

Mark's words came back to me last summer, as I thought about the meaning of the "scandals" over Father Bruce Ritter and Archbishop Marino. I'm one of those people who has considered these men to be contemporary heroes. In fact, I can remember, some months ago, saying to the parishioners where I live, "I'd be willing to bet my life that there's nothing to these accusations against Father Ritter."

Guess I should watch those bets, hunh! Or, maybe, I shouldn't. Is the wrong that people do so grievous that we should negate our feelings of admiration for the good they've also accomplished? And is it possible for us to continue, truly, to love the person while abhorring the evil deed they commit?

These questions haunt, I believe, many of us who had placed on pedestals people like Ritter and Marino. And yet, maybe, that's where Bavaro's insight takes on such meaning. Whenever we elevate human persons to the role of hero, we almost surely will be disappointed. Human beings fail. They blow it. They're not perfect. They often, even the best of them, have clay feet. So, to lionize any public figure is to set ourselves and them up for a fall. It makes more sense to focus on only one absolute hero, and his name is Jesus Christ.

Now, does all this mean that we can't or shouldn't admire and emulate the enormous accomplishments of Father Ritter and Archbishop Marino? Not at all. But let's not mistake affirmation of their accomplishments for the canonization of the individuals who do good. Let's not forget that beyond anyone's media hype are people who are probably part saint and part sinner.

Some years ago I met a man named Ian Charleson. He's an actor I had admired immensely. He played the role of the Scottish Olympic Gold Medal Winner in the 1981 film *Chariots of Fire*. His portrayal of purity and devotion to our Lord knocked me out. The movie still makes me cry. And to elevate further the feelings I had for this talented actor, his next picture was *Gandhi*. In it he plays a dedicated and committed minister who risks all for equality and justice. On top of all this, people who knew Charleson said he was a terrific human being. And so, even though he hadn't done much American-based cinema in the past decade, I continued to keep him high on my list of movie heroes. Until this past year, because during the month of April his death was announced. And he died of AIDS. Suddenly, he wasn't such a hero anymore. Suddenly his nobility seemed incongruous. How could this man who, on screen, shone forth such goodness and virtue, die from such an ignominious disease?

And then, thank God, I caught myself. Ian Charleson *was* a good man. He was not perfect, no one is, save God. But expecting him to be a saint is my blindness, not his.

Charleson, like Ritter and Marino, tried to do good. Sometimes they succeeded, at other times, probably failed. But they are still what we all are, beloved children of an awesome and compassionate God. And if he forgives all, who are we to condemn? And so, Ian Charleson, Father Ritter, Archbishop Marino, I apologize. I was wrong twice. I chose to make you heroes. And then I condemned you for failing to live like one. From now on, I'll try to love you like *people*, and look to but one person as a hero. And his name is The Christ.

January 22nd

Tommy called at around 5 p.m. "Hey, Father Jim, what are you doing tonight, want to hang out?" "Can't tonight," I responded. "I have to head East to give a pro-life talk. Do you want to come?" "Sure, beats staying home." And so off we went, stopping for a quick McDonald burger on the way. Tommy is 16. He is a non-stop talker, an attractive kid in personality and looks. A "success" with the opposite sex, he (like many teenagers) talks about "hitting on" girls a lot of the time. He is charming and somewhat irresponsible, and, like many of his peers, not very much in touch with the consequences of his actions.

I spoke that night to a group of young adults and their parents. Then they watched the powerful film produced by Dr. Bernard N. Nathanson called *The Silent Scream*. The movie, put together by a man who used to do abortions, simply shows what an abortion looks like. People complain that the film is hard to take. So is abortion.

When the lights in the auditorium came back on there was a stillness you could cut with a knife. The only sound heard was some sniffles. A dialogue then began. One teacher was obviously angry. She thought the film too emotional, too graphic. She was countered by a 17-year-old girl who stood to say, "Maybe we need real life pictures," and then she went on to say what truly matters: "I never really thought about what I would do if I became pregnant, but after seeing this movie I know that abortion could never be one of my choices."

During the ride home my talkative friend Tommy was uncharacteristically silent. Finally, several miles into our journey, he spoke. "Father Jim, you know I had sex a few times and I never really worried about it. I mean, I always figured that if anything happened I could always, you know, have it taken care of...but that movie wiped me out. I never thought of it as a real kid before. How can people do that?"

They do it, Tommy, because they too have been conned into forgetting that beyond talk of "a woman's body," or "personal choice," or "reproductive freedom," the life destroyed is a human person of infinite value and potential. Most people are not evil, they are ignorant. Abortion has become a word without meaning.

16

Tommy is like most people I meet. They have anesthetized themselves to a very uncomfortable reality. They have allowed abortion to become just another word for problem-solver.

Each January 22nd many of us gather in Washington, D.C., to walk for life. We are there as a way to say to a nation of Tommys: Please realize what is happening in America. Please know that we are destroying our own future. We are there to commemorate that day, years ago, when the Supreme Court, in a wildly flawed decision, said that a baby in utero has no right to life. In marching we hope to effect a change in the law, but for the immediate moment our hope is much simpler: to remind Americans today considering abortion that the choice for life is theirs.

Remember several years ago the horror and revulsion we all shared when ABC television's *The Day After* showed us the effects of nuclear war? Well, imagine this comparative tragedy: a terrible force is unleashed. It decimates the populations of Montana, North and South Dakota, Wyoming, Colorado, Kansas, Minnesota, Iowa, Oregon, Idaho, Nebraska and Utah. You see, that's how many Americans we have lost through abortion since 1973 — lives of infinite value known now only to God.

As we sadly remember and reflect on these years of senseless death, it might be good to consider the words of Dr. Nathanson in the closing moments of his film *The Silent Scream*. This modern St. Paul, who likewise persecuted and destroyed the beloved of our Lord, expressed the rationale for his conversion about unborn life this way: "Since the 1960s we have a science which is known as fetology, which has allowed us to study the human fetus. And all of those studies have concluded without exception that the unborn child is a human being, indistinguishable from any of us and an integral part of our human community.

"Now, the destruction of a living human being is no solution to what is basically a social problem. And I believe a resort to such violence is an admission of scientific, and even worse, ethical impoverishment. Somehow I refuse to believe that Americans, who have put men on the moon, can't devise a better solution than the resort to violence.

"I think we should all here and now devote ourselves to an untiring effort to devise a better solution, a solution compounded equally of love, and compassion, and a decent regard for the overriding priority of human life.

"Let's all, for humanity's sake, here and now, stop the killing!"

Show the Pictures

In the painful film *Eclipse of Reason*, Dr. Bernard Nathanson shows us a late-term abortion. The pictures are overwhelming. His movie focuses on the 130,000 late-term (second and third trimester) abortions performed in our country each year.

The movie opens with a narration by the Academy Award-winning actor Charlton Heston. Heston issues a significant challenge to the popular media. He reminds us that all kinds of medical surgery are shown on television and cable television each day. And yet, he chides, the most common operation in America is almost never shown: an abortion. What, he wonders, are we afraid of seeing?

I spoke recently with a well-meaning man who told me that while he agrees with the pro-life philosophy in principle, he "has reservations about some of the tactics used by the right-to-life movement." When I questioned his meaning he replied, "Well, like showing those awful pictures." I've heard this complaint before. Maybe it would be good to explore the question.

Let me make some observations for comparison: when I try to show a film like *The Silent Scream* or *Eclipse of Reason* (films which clinically show what abortion is) to high school or college students, I meet a lot of resistance, primarily from faculty members. The pictures of abortion, I am told, would be too upsetting: and yet, you and I know that these same students will be bombarded, in the course of a single day, by numerous acts of violence on television, in the movies and on cable. An evening of television, in fact, contains some six deaths (mostly violent, often bloody) on each major network station every day of the year.

Abortion, on the other hand, is a real violence most students don't actually comprehend. In an age of "pro-choice," why not let them see and know what they might well be choosing? Some teachers will respond that we may have students attending who have had an abortion, and the movie will be a painful reminder. That's true. But in my experience, far from hurting the woman (or her boyfriend), this experience usually pushes them to talk about it, to deal with it, to cope with it, not to bury it. Unfailingly, when I am around after a presentation, students stay to talk. And some want to talk about their own abortions. In many cases, they'd been denying what in their hearts they have always known, that something very wrong had taken place when they aborted; and they need to face it, seek the forgiveness of our compassionate God, and move on with their lives. That's my experience, not once or twice but dozens of times.

When I was in high school, we learned many important things about the value of human life. We saw pictures of the Nazi holocaust at Auschwitz and Buchenwald, and knew from the pictures genocide was a vile evil. Pictures showed us what no amount of words could tell.

I remember, too, through TV pictures, the brutality that accompanied the integration of our country. Watching people fighting for civil rights being beaten, hosed and bitten by police dogs was all we needed to know to recognize that racism is a corruption of all we are called to be.

Public television can educate so profoundly. I recall their program about the atomic explosions at Nagasaki and Hiroshima. The pictures of the blind, the burned, the maimed and the dead forced us to know that nuclear war costs too much, and that reasonable people can never resort to such unspeakable horror. And who can forget the pictures from Vietnam? Children racing down the road screaming in unbearable pain from the sting of napalm. The photographs of their agony-filled faces tore at our hearts, punctuating for us the futility of war.

Pictures teach us. They explain in language far surpassing ordinary prose. Photographs of abortion do upset us, as well they should. But our temporary queasiness is really no match for the indescribable pain felt by the victim of abortion: the innocent unborn child. People tell me that films about abortion are difficult. And I agree. But they don't hold a candle to the wrenching agony of being destroyed.

We should show the pictures and then let people make their choice. If they see what we are doing to children, they may well choose life.

"Don't Worry, Be Happy"

Carter Cooper had it all.

He was young, handsome, rich, well-connected, talented and famous. He was the son of Gloria Vanderbilt. He had what most everyone else wants. He had, as the expression goes, everything to live for.

But in July 1988, after battling months of depression and inconsolable interior pain, Carter checked out. In the presence of his pleading and shocked mom, Carter Cooper jumped off the balcony of their 14th floor apartment, falling to an instant death. His pain was, at last, over.

But for the people who loved him, the question of "Why?" would echo time and again.

In his leap to freedom from the emotional and psychic nightmares which robbed him of peace, Carter Cooper joined some 450,000 teenagers and young adults who attempt suicide each year. Somewhere between five and ten thousand young people "succeed."

The incidence of young persons trying to "off" themselves is growing tremendously. In the past 25 years, attempts at suicide have increased by 300 percent. And the depression that leads to suicide is an "equal opportunity" visitor. The poor, the rich, the middle class — all share in the downward spiral of despair.

In the early Church there were catalogues of serious sin. Certainly murder and sexual promiscuity were high on the list of moral wrongs. But right up there, at the top, was the sin of *tristitia* or despair.

The thinking of the Church elders was that if you really believed that Jesus saved us, then there should be no reason to despair. If you believe in the love of God, only rejoicing makes sense.

The problem is, there are a lot of people in our world who aren't so sure they are loved by God or by others. And even if they know that others love them, they have a really tough time loving themselves or allowing the love of others to really touch them.

The Carter Coopers don't just happen. When a young person attempts suicide there are usually reasons or causes for the desperation.

The most common cause is simply a need to escape. So many homes are torn apart by family crisis. We're living in a time with more divorce, separation, abuse (physical and emotional) and conflict than ever before. And in the middle of all this chaos and hurt, we've got less time to deal with our problems because of the frantic pace at which we lead our lives.

When a person experiences a need in our culture, there are many temporary means we use to achieve immediate and oftentimes superficial gratification. Drinking and drugging come to mind. Sexual release is another temporary remedy to alienation, loneliness or despair.

But the most alluring novocaine to pain or emptiness is sometimes seen as death. It's a way, some believe, to peace. Finally, they reason, the pain will go away. It seems to be an easier way to cope: the sleep of death rather than the struggle of pain, misunderstanding, loss and loneliness.

Sometimes, too, suicide becomes a way to strike back. When I have anger I can't express or people I can't reach, suicide is a way to communicate my frustration. People will, finally, take notice.

What do we do? Suicide is a dead end, and a senseless one at that. It causes us to lose some of the most sensitive souls around us. We need to be aware, before the death alternative is tried, of the warning signs of despair. (And most young persons *do* let us know that they're heading down that hopeless path.)

First, if someone says they're thinking about suicide, take them seriously. It's not true that the ones who talk about it never do it. They do.

Second, don't believe that only the wild child is thinking about suicide. Suicide happens among the "perfect" teenagers or young adults as often as it does among the drinkers, the drug-users or the school failures. In fact, heightened expectations about how well a person should succeed can set us up for an even greater fall.

Third, watch out for major personality changes. Zany or irrational behavior can be natural parts of growth and development. But huge movements toward dangerous activities, altered appetites, aggression, moodiness or withdrawal should send up red flags. Serious disturbances at home, at school or with the police shouldn't be ignored.

Take the clues seriously. Don't be afraid to seek professional help. Too many families believe that psychological counseling is only for "crazies." The truth is that sane and intelligent people recognize the need for outside help and get it.

Above all, remain calm and non-judgmental. If a son, a daughter or a friend is really depressed and shares those feelings with you, please don't be the dismissive jerk who says, "Well, we all go through that, you'll get over it." Or, "It's wrong to feel that way." Listen, support, affirm and steer the hurting person to

21

those who can help.

Some people who can assist you at times of crisis are The Samaritans. They operate a 24-hour hotline to aid people in despair. Their number is (212) 673-3000. Call them. They really can help.

A few years ago, a number-one song in our country was called *Don't Worry, Be Happy*. The fact that America made Bobby McFerrin's song a classic tells us a lot about ourselves. We really do want our world to be simple; to be happy; to hurt a lot less.

But sometimes, for all the upbeat songs, the pain *is* too much. Don't ignore the pain. Face it and get help.

Carter Cooper would have loved the song; he just couldn't live it.

When It Just Hurts Too Much

The recent spate of teenage suicides has been jarring my memory. I reflect back to my high school years and realize that for me, and for many others, they were years of sometimes painful growth.

They were times of disappointment. They were times of struggle with self-esteem. They were times less filled with real love than infatuation. They were definitely times when every personal crisis took on monumental importance. And even though parents, and older friends, and guidance counselors would say, "Don't worry, you'll look back on these times and wonder what all the fuss was about," it didn't diminish the way I felt.

And that was all right, because our feelings are *our* feelings. They're not right or wrong, they just are. And we're entitled to them. Having someone tell us that what worries us isn't really important doesn't make it any less intense or real.

Having an adult say that our feelings are "adolescent" or "immature" doesn't make us handle our crisis any quicker or better. No, it's probably best to accept the feelings we have and try to work with and through them.

And where the problems and feelings hurt too much, it's definitely best to share them with people who really care.

I got a call a while back from a girl named Janet. She had just turned sixteen. Janet had botched an attempt at suicide and wanted to talk over the forces that drove her to think about ending her life. After many hours the greatest of her needs surfaced: Janet, like the rest of us, needed very badly to be truly loved as a person instead of a thing.

In the year before her suicide attempt, Janet had been involved in two different relationships. Both led to sex. In both cases Janet admits that she thought that having sex would make the guys love her more. In both cases sex was actually followed by feelings of emptiness and of being used.

Janet said that the calls became less frequent after each sexual encounter. The terms of endearment both guys had used to coax Jan into bed were said less often. The attention they paid her generally was much less intense. And most frightening for

23

Janet was a feeling she developed about herself: she came to believe that her only real value was for sex.

The person she was inside — her feelings, her emotions, her sensitivities, her talents — was reduced or eliminated. Her self-image faded with every experience of sex. She was left, having just shared the deepest part of herself with another human being, feeling alone and empty. She said that she could be lying right next to the boyfriend of the moment and still feel an intense isolation which made her want to throw up.

Janet was hurting badly. And she felt that there were no avenues for communicating what she felt. Feeling poorly about herself led her to presume that anyone she spoke to would dislike her too. She was afraid others would judge her, condescend to her, put her down. And she just couldn't handle that. She was imprisoned by feelings of worthlessness and hurt. The pain was just too much.

One day Janet took pills, a lot of them. They almost killed her. Janet had finally given way to despair.

When Janet awoke at the local community hospital she didn't know how to feel. She was shocked to see her parents. They looked hurt, they looked worried, they looked angry, they looked relieved — all at the same time.

They told her that they were hurt that she hadn't felt free enough to confide her troubles to them. They said they were scared and worried because they almost lost a daughter they may not always like or understand, but whom they love very much.

They were also angry because that's how parents respond when they have no better way to express their pain. And they were hopeful, because they knew that they had a chance to try again.

Janet, her self-image and her family needed help. They now get the help they require. They sometimes find themselves wanting to give up because the experience of family counseling isn't always easy. But they don't. And maybe that's the key to the peace and the gentle smile you see on Janet's face more recently.

She knows that people care. She knows that she's not alone. She doesn't have all the answers, but she's no longer terrified of the journey toward self-discovery.

If you're feeling something like Janet — confused, or hurting, or isolated, or that the pain is just too much — please call for help.

There really are people who care. And looking to death instead of for a lifeline is such a tragic waste.

Let people who've walked out of the same darkness be a source of light and hope for you.

Because you matter too much not to.

Life Gives Hope

Father Ken Marks is one of my dearest and oldest friends. I have learned so much from him, especially about the quality of hope.

They say that when we are ordained, the first few assignments can have a lifelong impact on what kind of priests and Christians we are likely to be for the rest of our lives. Ken Marks' first assignment was in the South Bronx. It was a desolated, burned-out, depressing neighborhood.

When I heard that Kenny was assigned there I was concerned for him. He, to the contrary, was delighted. He saw the assignment as an opportunity to bring hope and love and help to people who were physically impoverished but spiritually powerful.

Kenny followed that assignment with a stint up in Harlem. The people in his parish had so little. They seemed to struggle just to survive. Again, in the midst of great human pain, Ken was illuminated by the opportunity to bring some joy, some strength and some dignity to the hurting and the needful.

Through our friendship Ken Marks often invited me and the people from my suburban parish to become involved in helping the good people of the South Bronx and the beautiful people of Harlem. And in a testament to our belief in the richness of giving over receiving, we always came home from Kenny's parish feeling grateful for the opportunity, in some small way, to make a positive difference.

One of the things which always struck me about Kenny and many of the Religious women and men who worked with him was their sparkling delight in the prospect of what these parishioners might yet hope to become. I never heard Kenny or the other generous people in ministry look with doubt as to God's purpose in creating the poor. They never allowed themselves to believe that it would be better for the poor if they had never been born.

Being Christian ministers meant that they were filled with hope and the joy of possibility. They recognized that the road out of vicious poverty would never be easy. They realized that often the people they worked with would climb the hill only to stumble again and again. But Kenny and his co-workers were empowered by a singular belief: if you are alive you can change, you can grow, you can be better.

There is hope where there is life, and my friend Ken saw the endless and spectacular possibilities that sprang from that simple reality: life contains possibility. Only death can quell that possibility.

I knew many of the young people, the old people, the sick people, the broken people, the uneducated people, the desperately poor people of Ken's parishes. With few exceptions they wished for more from life. They would certainly not have selected to be poor, given their druthers.

But I never knew one, not one, who would have wished not to exist. Given a choice, hurting as they could be, they always seemed to choose life.

It seems that when you work for and with the poor there are two roads you can follow.

One is the road of people like Father Ken Marks. You deal in life, and you know that where there's life, there's possibility, there's the chance to make things better.

The other road is one most often taken by the hopeless. They look at poverty and illness and joblessness and brokenness and they believe that the poor would be better off if they never happened. They are purveyors of doom. They have been swamped by the human hurt around them and have wished it all away.

They are the people who promote abortion and sterilization in neighborhoods like Harlem and South Bronx. They see the solution to black and Hispanic poverty as the elimination and termination of the people they can "save" from being poor.

It always struck me as odd that Kenny Marks, who is the ultimate social justice Democrat, is so resoundingly against abortion. And when I would ask him why he was so vehement against abortion, he would tell me, "Jimmy, people who really love the poor don't show their concern by destroying the people they claim to care about.

"If you hate the viciousness of poverty," he would say, "then help to make it better. Abortion is forever. Abortion kills. Abortion is a senseless and hopeless path to choose."

Sometimes the strongest advocates for abortion are those who work with the poor. I suspect that such persons are victims of the despair that, in confronting poverty, loses sight of the richness and possibility in life.

They apparently worked long and hard with the poor. And working in that part of society seems to push a person to see life either as an incredible gift or as a terrible burden.

Sadly these individuals have come to believe that they helped the poor by fighting for their right to destroy their own innocent, unborn children.

26

That is such a hopeless and empty solution. And in promoting such ultimate solutions, we can walk right past the reality of the most profound poverty of all — the absence of life.

Mother Teresa put it well when she said, "The poorest of the poor are not in my country (India); they are in places like America. Because in the midst of your wealth you do not see that the greatest poverty is to hate life. And abortion kills life. The poorest nations in the world are those who have abortion. That is the greatest poverty of all."

Coming Clean

You never forget your first car. I remember every detail about mine. It was a Chevrolet Nova, sky blue and beautiful. I couldn't afford it without some financial help from my parents. They were glad to pitch in, their only condition for assistance was that I "drive carefully!" Once, that warning was fine, but it became a common chorus every time I left the house. How foolish I thought they were. Why worry? Clearly, Nova and I were destined for a long and wonderful relationship, right? Wrong. Not fully two months after I got the car, disaster struck. I was heading home far too late from a long and exhausting high school reunion. I remember thinking: it would be nice just to close my eyes and rest for a second (a dumb idea when you're driving at 40 miles an hour). My next memory was seeing my car wrapped around another car. Nobody, thank God, was hurt. But poor Nova was history.

It took me a good day or so to call home from college. My mother was understandably upset. She told me that my father was away on business and suggested I call him with the news. "That won't be necessary," I said. "Why is that?" she asked. "Well, I'm not telling Dad about the accident." I don't remember exactly what my mother said in response, but the gist of it was: it's going to be kind of hard to explain the missing car over the next few years.

She was right. I had to come clean. I had to tell him. The next few days were awful. I worried constantly. I was sure my father would lose it. Certain that he'd chew me out. Convinced that he'd never help me again. I felt like a frightened, stupid fool. Three days after the conversation with my mother, with a knot in my stomach, sweaty palms and a huge tension headache, I called my father. Speaking quickly, I broke the news. Long pause. Dad responds, "Was anyone hurt?" "No." "All right, all right, relax, we'll talk about it when I get home." That was it. No screaming, no put-down, no "How could you be so stupid?" Just concern coupled with the sound of relief that no one had been hurt.

Too often we sell our parents short. We judge their limitations, and evaluate their coping abilities without giving them a real chance. Another example comes to mind. I had a visit one day from a young couple in the parish who I knew had been dating for about a year. When they came to see me, I could tell that something was making them incredibly tense. Finally, Valerie broke the news: "Father Jim, we're pregnant." I was happy for their expected child, if not thrilled with the way the baby occurred, but there were other challenges ahead. "Look, Father, Kevin and I love each other and we believe that it is wrong to get rid of the baby." I, obviously, agreed. "But Father, my parents don't even know that we've been fooling around; and if they find out that not only were we having sex, but that I'm pregnant, they'll kill me."

This was not the first time I'd heard about "parents who'd never understand." In most high schools I visit, the very first reason students give for why they'd have to abort is the fear of telling their parents the truth. Parents become the fall guys in this difficult situation.

I proposed to Valerie a possible solution for breaking the news. I would go with them. She agreed, and later that night we arrived at her parents' home. Her father was very warm and welcoming. At this point, he had no idea what the nice priest was doing in his home. But in the next half hour the tone of our visit would change.

True to Valerie's predictions, her father went crazy when faced with this unexpected news. He yelled, he cursed and he called her a slut. He promised to throw her out of the house. Meanwhile, her mother cried, and her boyfriend Kevin just kept quiet.

After many hours of hysteria, we called it a night. Valerie's dad stayed angry for about a month. He did not throw her out of the house. He stopped being angry, and then, gradually, he came around. He started to drive Valerie to the doctor, he nagged her about eating right, and he complained about her smoking, because "it would hurt the kid."

I have a final, perduring recollection about this family. When little Vanessa was born, I had the privilege of baptizing her. And when the christening was over, I stood at the back door of the church to say good-bye. The person who was lovingly cradling this beautiful baby in his arms was grandpa. His eyes were bright with gentleness and tenderness. For beyond the anger and the confusion and the pain of seeing his daughter make a mistake, he was what all parents strive to be: a good, caring and compassionate friend.

Friends like these should be given a chance. They deserve the risk of our trust, our honesty and our love.

We need to come clean with our parents. They're worth it!

Parents

I think that Matthew Broderick is a terrific actor. You will remember him in movies like *War Games, Ferris Bueller's Day Off, The Freshman,* and *Glory.* In one of his first films, *Max Duggan Returns,* he played a pretty normal teenager in a single-parent home. He enjoys a good relationship with his mom. They talk; they laugh, and they're honest with each other. My favorite scene, though, deals with the influence of peer pressure on our parental relationships. Matthew's mother is driving him to school. Normally, he would kiss her good-bye as he left the car.

But on this particular day she pulls up to a place outside the school where several of his friends are hanging out. Absurdly, he tries to shake his mother's hand to say good-bye. He doesn't want to look affectionate in front of his friends, at least toward his mom. His mother, beautifully played by Marsha Mason, pulls him right back in the car. She short-circuits his speedy departure to tell him that expressing love shouldn't end just because "the jerks are watching." It's a good lesson for Matthew and a timely one for all of us too.

These days are probably a good time to reflect on the relationships we have (or don't have) with our parents. Imagine someone giving us a monumental important responsibility for which you had little or no training. And the commitment isn't for a day, or a week, or a month, but for a lifetime. That's the situation for most parents. They don't go to school to learn how to do it right. They learn by doing. Now that means, at times, they will botch it badly; but at least they try.

As their children, we start out as totally dependent. We count on our parents for food, for shelter, for clothing, for laughter, and for comfort in sharing our fears. We especially count on them for love. Then something strange happens to us. We seem, for a few years, to outgrow the need for our parents. We begin to distance ourselves from them at the very time in our lives when we are most insecure, most in need of support, most vulnerable, and weakest in our self-esteem.

Our teenage years are, all experts agree, a time of transition and a period of awkward and lurching growth. We need stability and loyalty; at the same time we seem to run most quickly from

30

it. Suddenly the people who helped to bring us to this age are shunted aside and seen as irrelevant, or embarrassing, or ignorant of the world. Leaving them out is definitely a mistake. They have an insight, from being with us from the beginning, that no one else can have. They've learned, often from making mistakes, what we need and who we are. Shutting them out is a senseless waste.

All of it reminds me of my own high school years. I grew up being pretty open about expressing affection. Small children have a freedom about loving that isn't tainted by fear of what peers will think. And then, as adolescence took hold, I remember backing off from expressing love to my parents, especially my father. It simply wasn't macho or cool to kiss your dad. People (I thought) would look down on that.

Well, one day my dad and I were watching the Superbowl together. I was about 16. And the hero of the Superbowl-winning Jets was Joe Namath. Now, remember that "Broadway Joe" was reputed to be a lady killer. He was a true masculine stereotype. He was what everyone wants to be. Well, he wins the big one and goes back to the locker room to celebrate. All of his teammates are busy talking to reporters and popping champagne.

Joe, the star quarterback, doesn't. Instead, he wanders over to a corner of the room and literally picks up and hugs this little grey-haired man; then he plants a kiss on the man: his dad. In this moment of supreme joy, with the whole world watching, he wasn't afraid to demonstrate his gratitude and love to someone he treasured. I remember thinking, back in 1969, that if it's okay for Joe Namath, why should I be treating my father like a stranger?

From that time on, I have never missed the opportunity to show my dad and mom that I care. And, you know, beyond the first few times of expressing affection again, it really wasn't so hard to do. And the peers that I worried about, they're not around too much now. But my parents, thank God, still are. I'm really glad I didn't shut them out. They turned out to be the best friends I have.

Mothers

My mother recently underwent heart surgery. It's a tough operation, but one which increases the chances for a person suffering from heart disease. After they rolled her away to the operating room, a very sensitive old doctor came out and told us to go home. He'd call us when she came out of surgery. I went home, my father insisted on staying at the hospital. When you're waiting for someone you love to come through major surgery time seems endless. With nothing to do but think, my sisters and I started paging through old photo albums. And there, dating back to the 1940s and 1950s, were pictures of what our parents used to look like. They looked great. My mother was beautiful and in terrific shape. We don't usually think of our parents as good-looking, because they are, after all, our moms and dads. But here, page after page, we saw people of youth and zest and beauty.

Hours later the phone rang. Mom was out of surgery, and we could come to intensive care to visit with her for a few moments. Maybe we should have stayed at home. She looked awful, really beaten up. And the sound of the respirator drawing her breath in and out was a sound that ran right through me. As I stood by her bedside, my mind was drawn back to those earlier photographs. And I wondered: what had happened to that young and beautiful woman? What had helped her to become so tired and weak?

• Was it the burden of having children?

• Was it staying up all night with those children through measles, mumps, fevers, chicken pox, and all the other assorted ailments which plague children and burden mothers?

• Was it the thousand or so bundles of wash in an age before disposable diapers?

• Was it waiting for us to come home from dates, when our curfew was midnight but excuses always brought us in after 1 a.m.?

• Was it the people we dated who usually turned out to be every bit as bad as our parents had predicted?

• Was it the glassy eyes we averted or the alcohol on our breath (no matter how many mints we used to cover our drinking)?

• Was it our silly acts of rebellion when we rejected all

32

authority (including our parents) as outdated and stupid and out of touch?

- Was it Mom going without so that we would have more?
- Was it the vacation they didn't take because there were too many bills to cover?
- Was it all of those awful parent-teacher meetings, when teachers chided her children for unrealized "potential," but only Mom really believed that promise was there?
- Was it the times when her brothers or parents died, but there was so little time to grieve because we were children who needed to be raised?
- Was it the struggle to juggle the vocation of being a mother with the vocation of being a spouse?
- Was it the pain of letting go when we grew up, the challenge of loving us enough to let us be free?

Our parents give us so much, and it costs them. In the last episode of the long-running TV series *Family Ties*, Alex Keaton leaves his home to make a career in New York City. In the final scene between Meredith Baxter-Birney (Mom Keaton) and Michael J. Fox (Alex Keaton, her son), his mom expresses frustration. She tells him how hard it is to let a child go. So much pain, and work, and hope go into every child. And then, after a lifetime of loving, the truly healthy parent has to say goodbye. No easy task in that.

Our appreciation of our moms should not be limited to one nice day, Mother's Day. Our mothers are givers and, from time to time, we need to let them know that in a world sometimes devoid of heroes, they continue to give heroic witness.

In the hit song *The Wind Beneath My Wings*, Bette Midler sings about true heroes. She could well be singing about your mom or mine. It goes:

It must have been cold there in my shadow,
To never have sunlight on your face.
You were content to let me shine,
that's your way.
You always walked a step behind.
So I was the one with all the glory,
While you were the one with all the strength.
A beautiful face without a name for so long,
A beautiful smile to hide the pain.

Did you ever know that you're my hero?
And everything I would like to be.
I can fly higher than an eagle, but
you are the wind beneath my wings.

It might have appeared to go unnoticed,
but I've got it all here in my heart.

I want you to know I know the truth
because I know you.
I would be nothing without you.

Thank you, thank you, thank God for you,
The wind beneath my wings.

We take our mothers for granted too often. They are true heroes, they are the wind beneath our wings.

No Sacrifice At All

In the video for his latest best-seller song *Sacrifice*, Elton John offers a visual interpretation of his music. A man is left by his wife. She wants to head in new and more exciting directions. The man is left pining. He misses his spouse and longs for her return. But he's also got another need: he must raise their baby daughter alone. Throughout most of the video he seems overwhelmed by his situation. But by the end, as he dances with his little girl, the words, "It's no sacrifice at all" take on richer meaning. Because, in giving his time, his energy and his devotion to his daughter, he's discovered that sacrifice can really give meaning to life.

Another example comes to mind. Two young women, two responses. I was visiting a Catholic high school recently to speak about abortion. When I finished, a student rose to speak. She said words which haunted me. "Father, I agree with you that the unborn child is a person. But, well, I'm 18 years old, I have my whole life ahead of me. I want to go to college now. To be saddled with a child would be such a sacrifice." To which I responded, "That's true." And when another student suggested that a pregnancy could also lead to placement for adoption, yet another young woman rose to say, "It's really asking too much to expect a girl to carry a baby for nine months and then give it away." Another sacrifice too great.

The concept of sacrifice is growing steadily more unpopular. And yet, I don't know if it's even possible to love another human being unless I'm open to the reality of sacrificing. It costs to love. There's no such thing as love without surrender of my personal likes and wants for the sake of the mutual love.

I remember, about five years ago, trying to get my one-year-old nephew to sleep. I had no success. Every time I'd put him down in the crib he'd let out a wail. This went on for hours. At one point, when he was actually being quiet, I crept out of his room. I got the door open a crack when he let out the loudest scream yet. After what seemed like an eternity, he finally drifted off to sleep. I remember asking my mother, "Did we do that too?" "Of course," she replied. "How did you do it?" I asked. "You just love more than you care about the discomfort," my mother replied.

Everyone, it seems, wants to be a lover. But the path to true love is sacrifice. Think about it. Carrying a child for nine months is a sacrifice. Getting up at 5:30 a.m. every day to commute to a job you really don't like so you can pay your family's bills is a sacrifice. Shopping for your family for twenty years or so is no great joy. Holding a sick child's head over the toilet at 3 a.m. is no treat. Sitting up all night waiting for a maybe sober, maybe not, teenager is no special privilege. Changing the 4,000th diaper of a baby; removing the bedpan of an elderly parent; scrubbing the spastic child who suffers from cerebral palsy – none of these are activities any normal person would long for. And yet, every one of these actions says "I love you" much more powerfully than words.

And is it all worth the price, worth the sacrifice? Jodie DiFato thinks so. She's a 17-year-old woman with a child who's almost two. His name is James, and Jodie's raising him as a single parent. She spoke to a group of us recently about the challenge of parenting, about the lost sleep and curtailed plans, about the moments of frustration and the times when you just want to give up. And then, said Jodie, James gives you a smile or a hug. That's all. And suddenly, the sacrifice doesn't seem so bad. In fact, it's no sacrifice at all.

Can We Talk?

When she first called I thought it was a bad joke. She was nervous and there were too many pauses. I thought she was pulling my leg. She wasn't. In time she opened up and poured herself out, and I came to know that her story was very real and very familiar. She was 16 and pregnant and scared. She told me, "I heard you speak at my school last month, Father Jim, and I believe the things you said. I know that what's in me is a baby. It's real. I want it to live, I don't want to kill my child. But, Father, my parents don't know I've been fooling around with my boyfriend. They'll absolutely kill me if they find out I'm pregnant!"

Teenagers know a lot. Perhaps too much. They think that they know about love, but often it's more about lust. They really can delude themselves into believing that "this guy" or "that girl" is the one person they will love forever. And the self-deception can open the door to early and careless sexual activity. Fully 87 percent of the boyfriend/girlfriend relationships begun during high school do not last. But because hope springs eternal, everyone believes their love will be part of the special and lasting 13 percent.

Some argue that the answer to teenage sexual activity is more and better birth control (Planned Parenthood comes to mind). Accepting that mindset, however, is really saying: teenagers are not able to differentiate between right and wrong, so why bother trying to teach them? Contraception is no answer to what is essentially a matter of learning to use effectively our free will. Instead of surrendering to a contraceptive mentality, our teenagers would be better served if we let them know that they can say no, lovingly, to the boyfriend or girlfriend who insists that love is best proven by our willingness to have intercourse. Anyone who says that you must prove your love by "doing it" is really just a phony manipulator who is better avoided.

The key to teaching teenagers a responsible sexual morality is dialogue between parents and their children. In most major polls, parents indicate that they feel that they should be the primary teachers of sexual ethics for their children. Those same polls confirm that the vast majority of parents never talk directly about sex with their children. Somewhere in that inconsistency lies our problem. We need to challenge our children in direct ways about their sexual lives. And saying, "No, don't do it; it's bad," isn't good enough. We ought to be able to explain why. We need to approach teenagers and young adults in a positive and loving and open way. We need to tell children that sex is a beautiful gift of God meant to be shared responsibly by mature people who have the courage to make a life commitment to each other.

The girl on the telephone reminds us that we need to say something about the sacredness of life, the product of sexual sharing. We must explain that,while we do not want them to be sexually active before marriage, if they are and pregnancy results, abortion is never a moral or acceptable solution. Abortion only compounds the error of sexual involvement. Why can't we tell them that now, before it's too late?

Let's tell them what we believe. Let's remind them that they were God's gift to us, a gift we're so glad we never compromised. Let's tell them that if pregnancy occurs, they can rely on us. Let's assure them that as their parents (and as grandparents!) we can get through anything together so long as we're honest and straight with each other. Let's make it clear to them that we are the best friends they'll ever have. We really need, through dialogue, to eliminate the paralyzing fear of parents too many teenagers have. This fear, as I've discovered much too often in my ministry, drives thousands of our teenagers and young adults to the perceived "easier solution" of the abortion mills which in fact leaves our young people with guilt and pain and a deeply weakened self-image. Abortion is never an acceptable solution.

The girl who called me about her pregnancy asked me to go with her to break the news to her parents. I did. They did rant and rave. The father cursed a lot. The mother cried. They were both hurt and angry and confused. Their reactions, while hard to take, were a sign of their love and concern for their daughter. And once they exploded, they got over it. They love their daughter very much, and they demonstrated that love by standing by her.

Feelings did sometimes flair again. But the parents were faithful. They saw her through her pregnancy and gave her all the strength she needed to give life. Beyond the anger and disappointment which naturally comes with seeing someone you love burdened with serious responsibility, they were and are what all parents truly want to be: unconditionally loving friends for their children.

On Being Catholic and Proud

Imagine turning on your favorite station. You put up the volume to hear the tune they're playing. And instead of catching a song you can enjoy, you are dumbstruck to hear the singer deliver three minutes and 20 seconds of insult, put-down, invective and bigotry about someone you love. Sounds outrageous, right? But that's what I caught on a popular radio station this week.

It was an old song called *Only the Good Die Young*. The singer was Billy Joel, one of our richest and most popular music men. The target of this meanness, the person I love, was the Catholic Church. In this (relatively) short hit, Joel manages to condemn Catholic girls for remaining virgins, makes fun of the sacraments of Communion and Confirmation, insults those who pray the rosary, and promotes a classic case of anti-Catholic bigotry.

Later in the day I called the radio station which had played *Only the Good Die Young*. And after protesting their insensitivity to our beliefs, I asked the station manager if he'd received other calls about the song. He hadn't. "After all," he said, "the song is old, Joel came out with that song years ago." Translated: old bigotry is less damaging than new bigotry.

Well, then, let's consider some other anti-Catholic prejudice. *Newsday* is the biggest newspaper on Long Island. It's owned by the *Los Angeles Times* Syndicate. It's no secret that our Church must constantly fight for fairness from this mega-corporation. An example, somewhat subtle, comes to mind.

A boy from Ronkonkoma is accused of murdering a teenage girl. The crime is terrible, nobody is disputing that. But as *Newsday* paints a picture of this young man's background, they feel the need to add a little color. Describing the home in which the accused killer lives, the reporter highlights the fact that on the front lawn of his home stands a statue of the Blessed Virgin Mary. The inference is clear: look at those crazy Catholics, their children kill while they pray.

I wondered as I read the article, can you imagine *Newsday* printing a story and focusing on the Jewishness of an accused murderer? Can you envision an article which coupled a person's race with his or her criminal behavior? No way!

The newspapers or radio stations or television conglomerates which dared to link another religious belief with criminal action would rightly be brought to task. Why, then, do we as Catholics let these bigots get away with doing it to us?

Our traditions, our values, and our beliefs need to be guarded and defended. Too often, the popular culture and media can work to undermine the ideals we hold dear. A mega-hit movie comes to mind. Most young Catholic people I know flocked to the movies to catch the trendy *Dirty Dancing*. It remains a big hit in video rental and on cable. People said they enjoyed the dancing; others the music; some even fell for the stars, Patrick Swayze or Jennifer Grey. But consider the plot. A plain-Jane teenager (Jennifer Grey) undergoes a "growth-filled" summer. She becomes the movie's heroine. And not just because she learns to dance well. Not just because she lands (and sleeps with) Patrick Swayze, but also because she is "courageous" enough to milk her father for the money she needs to pay for a friend's abortion! Some heroine! She's viewed as having "grown" by helping someone kill. And millions of young people smilingly leave movie theatres around the country, humming the tunes (*I've Had the Time of My Life, Hungry Eyes, She's Like the Wind*) without recognizing that we've been brainwashed. With great smoothness the film-makers have sold us a bill of goods about what makes us truly attractive. In this movie you can be popular if you just sleaze around, lie to your parents, or pay for someone's abortion. A wonderful story, isn't it!

This film and many others like it join Billy Joel and biased newspaper reporting in eroding our sense of who you are and what you stand for. Their message is "dressed up" to be mainstream, popular and acceptable. And because Catholics (like everyone else) want to "fit in," we can sometimes go along, uncritically, and buy into the bigotry these songs and movies and media promote.

It's never too early in our lives to stand up for the people we love. And one person who needs our help and protection is our Mother the Church. As a teenager or young adult, you share in the special responsibility of taking on the bigots who mock and insult the Church, which is your spiritual home. If you'd like to get more involved in speaking up for the Church we love, why not write to The Catholic League for Religious and Civil Rights, 111 Presidential Blvd., Suite 227, Bala Cynwyd, PA 19004.

They'll be glad to send you information and ideas about what you can do to help the Church in America in resisting prejudice, ignorance, and bigotry.

Please get involved.

We Are Not Alone

Not long ago I was invited to participate in a debate about abortion. The local state university campus wanted to present both sides of the issue, and I was to make the pro-life case. Many of my friends urged me to decline. The campus is fairly liberal, and I was reminded that most of my audience would identify themselves as "pro-choice." Several students were kind enough to tell me that I would certainly encounter some very hostile questions. None of this bothered me much: pro-lifers don't usually place first in popularity contests anyway. I just hoped to change a few hearts and minds.

Standing at the podium of that debate engendered a feeling of incredible isolation. You feel as if no one shares your perspective about life. And you wonder, on such occasions, does anybody hold this vision? Is the horror of abortion only horrible for some of us?

The answer, I've come to see, is clearly no. Millions of normal mainstream, intelligent and sensitive people care about the unborn. Four out of five Christian Churches name it a "tragedy." Few are really comfortable with the reality of what abortion is. In one recent poll 58 percent of those surveyed called it "murder." Oddly, almost the same percentage said they wanted what they had just called murder to remain "safe and legal."

There are other notable voices who have spoken out against abortion. These are famous people you know, but whose opinions about abortion are well hidden by the secular press. Oh, they'll tell you about the "pro-choice" efforts of Jane Fonda, Glenn Close, Joanne Woodward or Cybil Shepard. But they never seem to mention those notables who are repulsed by abortion. Let me mention a few.

Well, there's Princess Diana. When asked to name her favorite charity she identified Birthright. Birthright, as you may know, is a non-sectarian program offering realistic alternatives to abortion. And Jack Nicholson. This two-time winner of the Academy Award was born to a teenage mother. His mother never married his father. He rejects the label "pro-choice." He says the choice is a choice to kill. And he thinks that it's wrong to destroy children. He says he knows that were he conceived in 1990 by a

41

poor, teenage single parent like his mother, he might well be another abortion statistic. Says Nicholson, "I'm positively against abortion. My only emotion is gratitude, literally, for my life."

And Mia Farrow. This talented actress who has a large brood of children (half of them adopted) minces no words about abortion. "Abortion is an issue that transcends all else. Life is life, and to kill is to kill, that's all." And her dedication to the children has borne fruit. The father of her latest child is film director Woody Allen. Formerly "pro-choice for a lack of adequate information," says Farrow, Allen now identifies himself as pro-life.

Then we have good people from the world of sports. Rosey Grier, a retired NFL football star, says, "God is the author of life. He is not the author of death. We must stop the murder of little innocent children." He's joined by Tom Herr of the New York Mets, who tells us, "We have permitted the daily killing of more than 4,000 innocent pre-born children. The self-serving, humanistic theories that have permeated our lifestyles have so eroded the moral fiber of our country that we rationalize away abortion. We fail to consider that what has been terminated is a human life."

In her powerful autobiography actress Gloria Swanson says of her abortion, "The greatest regret of my life has been that I didn't have my baby. Nothing in the whole world is worth a baby." In this sentiment she echoes actress Patricia Neal and countless others who regret the tragedy of abortion.

Peacemakers throughout this century have also spoken eloquently about abortion. Consider the words of Mahatma Gandhi: "It seems to me, clear as daylight, that abortion is a crime." His words resonate with the same power as Nobel Peace Prize winner Mother Teresa: "I feel the greatest destroyer of peace today is abortion."

And don't forget the "stars." Mel Gibson, Helen Hayes, Brooke Shields, Kirk Cameron, Robert Blake, Kevin Costner, Tom Selleck, Martin Sheen, Pat Boone, (author) Ken Kesey, Merle Olsen (*Little House on the Prairie*), Lisa Whelchel (*Facts of Life*), Denice Williams, Jordan Knight (*New Kids on the Block*), and Charlton Heston, all oppose abortion. Heston explains why. "Abortion is the ultimate act of violence. Since 1973 abortion has claimed millions of mute and innocent victims. The silence has to stop."

Even a character like Madonna, for all her misguided sexual politics, isn't so lost as to forfeit the unborn. Says the singing superstar, "I know I offend people. But those who understand me are not offended, they know what I stand for. I'm pro-life, pro-equality and pro-humanity."

Back to our debate. It went well. There was hostility, but the students mostly listened. And slowly, with an occasional nod of the head or an agreeing smile, I could see the message starting to register. We who speak for the unborn are not alone. We have not only the noted in our camp, but countless others who, with a fundamental sense of human decency, understand that the killing must stop.

Champions of Life

Recently, through the course of one week, I clipped out every article in the newspapers and magazines about professional athletes. Most stories centered on scores, games won or lost, drug testing, drug busting, contracts negotiated, bucks offered and bucks refused, holdout strikes and sexual piccadilloes. One article out of a hundred highlighted the good and altruistic side of the men and women in sports. That one piece was about former football star Roger Staubach and the needed work he does as director for the Special Olympics.

You know, it's a shame. More and more we read about athletes who seem to be preoccupied with material success to a self-centered degree. Too often these contemporary stars are seen as takers instead of givers. And that's particularly disappointing when polls and studies tell us that professional athletes are true heroes and heroines for America's young people. Watch the faces of children or teenagers or young adults when there's an athlete around. They gaze starry-eyed at these modern day supermen and superwomen. Makes you wish that more of these talented folks could cast their lot with the generous, the caring, the giving and the life affirming. Wouldn't it be wonderful if one of these baseball card autographing gatherings were done to help the needy instead of the promoters?

Well, it's happening. In the past two years a group of athletes has started to work specifically for the weakest, the most defenseless, the oppressed, the tormented and the most innocent members of our society, namely, the unborn.

Inspired by the owner of the New York Giants football team, Wellington Mara, and implemented by the American Life League's Dick Reeder, Athletes for Life is expanding rapidly. Its members are successful stars from the world of professional baseball, football and golf who have one common vision: they all think it's wrong to destroy innocent unborn life. What is especially surprising about these athletes and their devotion to the pro-life cause is that they reap no material rewards for their involvement. And, actually, they risk alienating the pro-abortion secular media who can and do make and break careers. Abortion is no safe or easy issue. To stand for pre-born life can cost. And

44

yet these daring spokespersons for God's defenseless children take the risk. And why do they do it? Well, it's well explained in their new video film called *Champions for Life*. Members of the championship New York Giants football team speak out on the issue and clearly explain their choice for life.

Says Mark Bavaro: "Thanks to God and my parents who gave me the greatest gift of all, life. I wonder how many future champions will be killed before they see the light of day?"

Says George Martin: "The Supreme Court said unborn babies have no rights. Roe vs Wade legalized the destruction of babies. It was just as shameful as the Dred Scott decision, which said black people have no rights. I hope you will help right this terrible wrong."

Says Phil McConkey: "As long as you have life in you, you've got a chance. When you take the life of a baby by abortion, it will never have a chance."

Says Phil Simms: "Over 4,400 babies are killed every day by abortion, or 1.6 million killed every year. My statistics as an athlete seem very insignificant by comparison."

Says Chris Godfrey: "Every twenty seconds an American baby is killed by abortion. Since Roe vs Wade, over 25 million American babies have been killed – one every twenty seconds."

And each of these athletes is reflecting the thoughts of a wide cross section of humanity up until a few years ago. The preamble of the United Nations Declaration on the Rights of the Child reads, "The child needs special safeguards and care, including appropriate legal protection before as well as after birth."

Too often the news about sports figures is negative. It's great to know about the courageous message of Athletes for Life.

(To secure a copy of the video film *Champions for Life*, send $10 to The American Life League, P.O. Box 1350, Stafford, VA 22554.)

Interfaith Marriage

The ghettos are disintegrating. The neighborhoods which once held us into categories of race and creed are no longer realistic possibilities. In our religiously homogenized society there are fewer and fewer "neighborhoods by religion." The family next door may be Catholic, but might just as easily be Protestant, Moslem or Jewish.

And even if our neighborhoods are still all Catholic, our young people, through high school and college, will mix with ever widening religious perspectives. Interfaith marriage is here to stay. Whereas a decade ago only ten percent of our young people selected a partner who was not Catholic, now the percentage has jumped to 32 percent. And the increase is fraught with difficulties that couples will need to confront early in their engaged and dating relationships.

It is no accident that more (by 12 percent) interfaith couples end their relationships in divorce than those marrying a person of the same faith. It takes a couple willing to confront a variety of pitfalls and differences to make interfaith marriage work. In the sections below, I will attempt to outline some of the challenges, and possible solutions, to the interfaith marriage issue:

1. Love doesn't conquer all. Many interfaith couples know that there are serious differences between their two faiths. They recognize that the differences aren't going to go away, but they sincerely believe that love offers a surefire balm for every potential problem. It doesn't. The differences must be dealt with early and openly. The ostrich route is no solution. Love is a wonderful thing, but it cannot be used to replace dialogue and discernment.

2. "Aren't we really all the same, anyway?" Some people become ecumenical like nobody's business when they meet and fall in love with a person of another faith. They ignore the religious, the cultural and the traditional hurdles in favor of a view of all religions as "essentially the same." To deny our differences is naive at best. We are the products of highly varied theological backgrounds and points of view. We were immersed in these beliefs at a tender and formative age. We are not likely to sweep away our long-held beliefs and traditions too easily. Nor should we. When we fall in love with someone, we love all that the person is, and we need to recognize that our Catholic, or Jewish, or Protestant upbringing helped to shape the person we love into that particular human being. To erase the differences or make believe that they don't exist is to deny a part of who and what we are.

3. Dispensations matter. We went through a time when couples living together would argue that marriage is "just a piece of paper, a legality." There is a similar tendency towards Church dispensations as well. To marry a person of another faith, the Catholic partner needs to sign a dispensation. This promise states that because his Catholic faith means so much to him, he will do all in his power to have their children baptized and reared as Roman Catholics.

A second dispensation is filled out if the couple wishes to be married outside of a Catholic church. A Catholic/Protestant couple may be married in the church of either family. A Catholic/Jewish couple may celebrate their wedding in a Catholic church; in a Jewish synagogue; or in a neutral setting (e.g., an interfaith chapel, a catering hall).

The dispensation is a controversial item. Some view it as a way of exerting control over the religious destiny of children. It isn't meant to be a control issue at all. When we celebrate a Baptism, we are fundamentally saying two things. First, that we want our child to know Jesus. We are saying that our child's life would be infinitely poorer if he were to go through life without understanding the joy, the compassion, the forgiveness, the friendship and the life-saving goodness of a relationship with Christ. We are also saying that we want our child to belong to a community of faith. We want our children to have a particular direction and sense of identity. We want for our children, wherever they go in life, to know that they have a home in the Catholic Church.

Like the purposes of Baptism, the dispensation is a way of committing our children to a particular religious direction. It doesn't preclude the full knowledge of the non-Catholic spouse's faith. It is just saying that life is filled with particular choices, one of which is, "What faith will I learn and try to live?"

Some argue that a child should be directed to no particular faith but be made aware of all faiths and decide on a particular faith in adulthood. That sounds good but it's not very practical. Any parent who has tried to teach even one faith well knows that it's an oftentimes overwhelming task. To offer your child a religious smorgasbord is much harder to accomplish than couples might realize.

Another compromise practiced by some couples is the notion of bypassing the religion of both husband and wife and raising the child in a neutral "third religion." While that might seem "politic," it is really ignoring the richness of two already developed faiths in favor of a third, about which nothing is known. It tends to further separate families already grappling with religious differences. Instead of two divisions we now have three.

Some couples, in an attempt to bypass the critical impact of a dispensation, will dismiss it as "just one more Church rule." Many sign the promise intending to ignore its conditions. Sadly, even some priests attempt to minimize the requirements of the dispensation. Filled with a desire to be "nice guys," priests can water down the meaning of the promise.

That's really a dishonest disservice to the engaged couple. A promise is what we have always known it to be: the giving of our word. We place our very lives in the words we promise. And if our words are untrue, so are we.

You may recall in the powerful drama, *A Man for All Seasons*, that St. Thomas More is encouraged by his daughter Lady Margaret to tell King Henry VIII what he wants to hear. More is advised by his daughter that he should keep in his heart his true beliefs, while telling the king that he agrees with him. St. Thomas responds by saying, "When a man takes an oath, Meg, he's holding his own self in his own hands." We have only our word. When a man stands beside a woman before the altar of God and promises "to love and honor you all the days of my life," he is giving his word, he is giving his promise. A wife is impelled to trust and believe. So, too, the Church trusts and longs to believe in the sincerity of the Catholic who seeks a dispensation to marry a person of another faith. Please, do not promise what you will not try to live.

4. Conversion is between God and you. To "streamline" religious differences, people sometimes encourage their intended to convert. It's thought that this will eliminate any conflicts or problems. But that's like deciding what someone's relationship with God will be, without asking God what he thinks. Conversion is a spiritual journey. It isn't a political decision to achieve peace at any price. We can't legislate a religious belief for our spouse. The person we love must be called, not pressured, into embracing a particular faith. If freely chosen, faith can be a wonderful gift. If force-fed, it can be an uncomfortable albatross of little meaning or purpose.

5. Love and respect your parents, but marry your spouse. It has always been the teaching of our Church that the primary relationship in marriage must be between a husband and wife. No one and no thing must get in the way of that bonding. Oftentimes, with the best of intentions, our parents attempt to play a major role in the issues that an engaged couple must face within interfaith marriage. Our parents, who may not have been the most devout Catholics, or the most devout Protestants, become terribly interested in religion when it looks like their grandchild isn't going to be of the same faith. We can

48

become very territorial about our religion when we sense an alien presence. The engaged couple must make whatever decisions need to be made with a sense of respect and even reverence for their parents. But the ultimate decision must be their own.

Interfaith marriage is becoming much more commonplace and acceptable. It is, however, still no easy hurdle. It requires much dialogue and honesty between the engaged. It can, with openness, even become an advantage. Most Catholics don't dialogue much about the role of religion in marriage. They presume that it will play a role, but leave that role undefined. Interfaith couples don't have that luxury, they must talk about it and use their hearts and minds to make serious concrete decisions. In this, interfaith couples are experiencing, perhaps, their first "working through" of a marital challenge. Interfaith marriage can work, but only with a powerful sense of devotion, mutual respect, dialogue and sensitivity.

Self-Esteem

In his first hit album singer-songwriter Richard Marx belted out a cynical hit called *It Don't Mean Nothing.* The theme of the song reflects Marx's belief that the world around us is filled with hypocrites, phonies and users. In particular he's talking about Hollywood, Los Angeles and the music industry. His warning, though, has meaning for everyone. He advises us not to fit our beliefs or values into the neat package that'll make us popular or acceptable to others: he warns us that being successful can cost us our souls.

I thought of Richard Marx during the last Winter Olympics at Calgary. If there were "stars" at these Olympics they would surely be Pirmin Zurbriggen, the Swiss downhill ski racer who took home the gold, and Dan Jansen, the speed skater who did not. Both of these outstanding young Catholic Christians are individuals who hold to beliefs and convictions that demonstrate courage and self-esteem.

Consider Pirmin. How many young, good-looking, successful, talented people do you know who talk freely about their devotion to Mary, the Blessed Mother? Pirmin does. He's been to the Shrine of Our Lady of Lourdes five times as a sign of his commitment to the Mother of God. Without embarrassment he carries with him a picture of Mary wherever he goes. He prays each day. He thanks God for his goodness and he asks God for his blessing and protection. He goes to Mass regularly, with his mother no less! And he doesn't care whether you think he's cool or not. He believes. He practices what he believes and the only person he worries about pleasing is God.

Consider, too, Dan Jansen. He took everything we see as important, namely winning, and showed us success in failure. He lost in every race, but lost with dignity. He was a winner just by competing in the midst of sorrow over the death of his beloved sister. He showed the world grace and style. He showed us that it's okay to cry in front of the whole world when you're hurting. In what the world would call failure, he demonstrated greatness. In a world which makes heroes of the macho, Dan had the courage to cry.

What Dan Jansen and Pirmin Zurbriggen showed us was what

it means to have true self-esteem. Self-esteem means believing in yourself. It means that you know that when God made you he knew what he was doing. It means having the confidence to follow your beliefs even when others laugh at you. It means having the courage to be religious in an irreligious world. It means that looking cool isn't nearly as important as being true. It means being solid enough to cry freely and openly. It means the opposite of being trendy. It means that clothes aren't anywhere near as important as the person inside them. It means knowing who you are and believing that who you are is good.

A few years back I met a couple who were engaged to be married. And although they said all the "right" things, something about the girl made me wary about their relationship. So one day I made a point of seeing her alone and asking her about the way they related. I remember that she started to cry. She then told me some really frightening stories about the physical and emotional abuse her fiance was heaping on her. When she was finished I told her that I thought that marrying any clown who'd hurt her in those ways was a disaster. And I told her that I could never participate in a wedding ceremony uniting her to someone so destructive. She became frantic. "But we have to get married," she said. "Why?" I asked. "Because," she answered, "he's the best thing I'm going to find."

This young woman had little or no self-esteem. She really believed that she deserved so little happiness. In some way she probably believed that she deserved his abuse. No one does. And no one should take it. We're, all of us, worth much more than that.

What Pirmin Zurbriggen knows, what Dan Jansen knows is that everyone of us is made in the image and likeness of God. He believes we're very special. If we don't believe that too, aren't we really calling God a fool?

Being Consistent

I had a wonderful opportunity recently to meet a very impressive young man named Robert Townsend. He's a film director, a writer, an actor, and a comedian. He's also a creative juggler. In order to finance his first film *Hollywood Shuffle*, he borrowed against a bunch of credit cards, which gave him the $50,000 he needed to finish his movie. Robert's cleverness really paid off. The film was a critical and popular success, and the media appreciated his daring ways of producing his dream.

Townsend also starred in his own HBO comedy special, and it, too, was well received. His most notable success to date is the movie he directed called *Eddie Murphy Raw*. It's made tons of money for all concerned. I mention this because during the five hours we spent together this gifted "rising star" of the entertainment world really impressed me. He is gracious and gentle. He is sensitive and thoughtful. He is openly dependent on God, and feels a deep awareness of the Lord's presence in his life. He is close to his family, and clearly loves his mother. Townsend has great compassion in his eyes, and is truly grateful to God for all of his good fortune. He is a fine Christian gentleman.

About a week after meeting this delightful man, I found myself with friends who wanted to see a movie. One of them mentioned the hit *Eddie Murphy Raw*. Now, I know about Eddie Murphy's propensity for crassness, but I was open to the idea of seeing the film. Why? Because I had met the good man who had directed it. And good as he is, how bad could his movie be?

Answer: really bad. The movie respects no one. Murphy has the foulest mouth I have ever heard. His routine is less comic than filthy. And even Murphy's fellow comedian Billy Crystal has identified Eddie Murphy's style less as comedy than as abusive insult masquerading as humor. Murphy reduces every person at whom he takes aim. And he does it crassly. He takes the God-given gift of human sexuality and reduces it to a toilet level object. He focuses all of his humor on the chest and the crotch, and forgets that people have hearts and minds too.

I walked out of the theater disgusted, annoyed and feeling betrayed. Maybe betrayed is the wrong word. Maybe confused would be better. How, I thought, could a good and sensitive and caring man like Townsend preside over something which reflects none of his previously sound beliefs?

Each of us owns a dresser. If you pull out the top drawer, most dressers have slots or compartments for storing different articles of clothing. Socks in one section, shirts in another. And that works fine for clothing. But we can also set up compartments in our lives. We can compartmentalize our daily living instead of seeing all parts as homogeneous. Who we are and what we believe should directly influence what we say and do. If, as a priest, I get up and preach every Sunday about tolerance, compassion, generosity and forgiveness, but on Monday treat others like dirt, then my life is a hopelessly divided contradiction.

Our brains, our hearts, our God-life and our bodies are all tied together. And if our spirits are in one compartment while our bodies lie in another, then we're inconsistent and false.

What Robert Townsend did, we all do. We separate who we are from what we do. Let's bring it together. Our hearts will rest easier if we do.

A Family Perspective

In a moving and symbolic action, many brides and grooms have added something new to their wedding ceremony. Following the exchange of vows and rings, they take two long stemmed roses and leave the altar to give these flowers to their parents. It's a wonderful way of saying "thank you," a moving way of saying "I love you." And it really recognizes the reality of love's source. No bride or groom would be able to love each other unless they first learned the meaning of love from others who chose to love them. And, for most of us, our first understanding of love comes from our homes.

Love is not all we learn in our families. We also learn or fail to learn about the importance of respecting and treasuring all life. No 16-year-old teenage girl wakes up to find herself pregnant without having been shaped by a particular set of values given to her by her family. Similarly, no young man who helped to get his girlfriend pregnant comes to his moment of decision about supporting or deserting the mother of his child without reflecting the values he learned within his family. Family is the source (and substance) of the way we see the world. Our values, our loves, our hates, our priorities and our principles are shaped by the people with whom we live.

What condition, then, do we find the American family in? And how does the state of our families impact on respect life concerns?

Consider these facts:

• Our nation is the most marrying country in the world, with the highest divorce rate to match.

• We view ourselves to be a society of "traditional" values and yet, we often do not match, in fact, our own self-vision. For example, by 1985 only seven percent of our families were still living the traditional situation of a father working, a mother staying at home to raise the family, and there being more than one child. Instead, over 48 percent of mothers with infants one year of age are out working and over 70 percent of mothers with school-age children are working outside the home.

• Twenty-five million children return from school to homes where parents are away because of the need to work.

54

- The four-generation family is now the norm in the United States, which means that family concerns will encompass all aspects of life from infancy to the aged.
- The image of the solid, "Catholic home" is also changing, as interfaith marriages increase rapidly. Catholics are being married to non-Catholics at a rate twice that of their parents.
- The desire to live outside the family is also increasing. In the decade from 1970 to 1980 there was a 64 percent increase of persons living alone.
- The old homestead is also ever-changing. From 1970 to 1980 over 50 percent of Americans changed their residences.
- Divorce is epidemic. From 1901 to 1987 divorce increased by over 700 percent in the United States. This year alone at least one out of every three first marriages will end in divorce. If you add in remarriages, the ratio increases so that one in every two marriages this year will end in divorce. And how are our children affected by this divorce rate? Consider these realities:
- Fifty percent of children whose parents divorce do not see the non-residential parent from one year to the next.
- Only one child in six has regular weekly contact with his or her father following a divorce.
- Ten years after divorce, 75 percent of children never see the non-custodial parent.
- Over one-fourth of the children in America now life in single-parent households. That percent will rise to 60 percent before most children graduate from high school because of divorce, out of wedlock birth, or the death of one parent.
- And then, consider the issue of poverty brought about by this disintegration of American family life:
- Ninety percent of women who divorce take custody of their children, while losing some 73 percent of their annual income. Men, on the other hand, improve their income following divorce by some 42 percent.
- Twenty-five percent of fathers do not make a single child support payment after divorce. This leaves millions of women and their children living well below the national poverty line.
- One out of four preschool children lives in poverty.
- One-third of our nation's children will live on public assistance before they reach their eighteenth birthday.
- One out of every five children is now born out of wedlock. That is an increase of 50 percent in the last ten years.
- Between 1970 and 1980 there was a 157 percent increase in people (unmarried) living together.
- At least 2.5 million children are the victims of domestic violence each year.
- Twenty million children live with at least one alcoholic parent.
- Over a million children run away from home every year. Many survive through the promotion of prostitution and drugs.

• The suicide rate among teenagers has more than tripled in the past two decades.

I mention these facts not to alarm people, but to indicate our need to rebuild and reaffirm the American family. It should come as no surprise to us that life has become cheap. The fundamental support for a pro-life value system has always been solid family living. If our families are no longer intact, and are, in fact, deeply wounded, how can we expect an appreciation of the sanctity of life to flourish?

Family Perspective II

I've outlined some of the more significant challenges facing contemporary families. Let me attempt here to suggest several possible solutions to the crises we face:

See family as domestic Church. We need to see the people in our family as sacred. There is a need to diminish the cold and, at times, boiling warfare which fills our homes. When people come to me in confession, I often confront family wars through the penance I ask. I request that for one solid week they should say only what is positive, supportive and affirming to family members. They are asked to use the gift of speech to build up, not tear down. This would (if followed) eliminate cursing, nagging, swearing, put-downs, envy, sarcasm and rudeness within our homes.

Repudiation of all violence. Hitting, slapping, kicking another member of the family is a sickness. The person who hits a family member in violence needs help. But he or she does not deserve or require the cooperation of martyrs. At the first sock in the jaw, the sane spouse should draw the line. Putting up with domestic violence is almost as disturbing as perpetuating such violence. Do not cooperate with a person's illness by lying down and playing doormat. Challenge the oppressor to get help or get out.

Divorced men — shame on you! A failed marriage is not a license to deprive your wife and children of their financial and emotional support. It is tragic that men continue to punish their families following a divorce by failing to pay court-ordered support or being unwilling to visit the children they helped to create. The reality of poverty among divorced women with children is a striking indictment of men's self-centeredness. Failing to pay child support is another form of child abuse. The wounds are social, but they hurt as surely as if a father kicked his child in the stomach.

Alcohol and drug abuse require help. No one in our family should ever be blamed for being an alcoholic or drug abuser. Alcoholism and related abuse is a disease. Disease left unchecked destroys family life. We cannot blame someone for being ill; we can judge them harshly for failing to seek help.

Sexism in the kitchen. Women are no longer limited to life around the home. They work as long and as hard as men do (and often for less money). It is insensitive in the extreme to expect a woman to work all day outside the home and then perform around the home as if the house was her only concern. Shopping, cleaning, cooking, doing laundry, scrubbing bathrooms and changing diapers are not properly male or female jobs. They are simply necessary for domestic order. If both parents work, these tasks should be evenly shared.

Child abuse is never acceptable. There are two kinds of illnesses in a home scorched by child abuse. The first sickness involves the person who lashes out at his child because internal peace is absent. The second illness rests with the second parent who allows such abuse to continue. The scars of child abuse last a lifetime. They are everyone's concern.

Poverty is everyone's problem. The impoverished single-parent family living in the next village will, sooner or later, directly impact on me and my family. We are naive to believe that we can live in a fortress of safety from the realities of poverty and the resulting despair, criminal activity, drug incidence, and the fostering of racial and ethnic hatreds. Helping the poor to achieve a greater spirit of dignity is the concern of every citizen. The growing rate of infant mortality among the poor is a serious crisis which should shame us and compel us to do more.

Divorce — a painful reality. Divorce used to be a closeted reality in "nice" Catholic families. It is no secret anymore. We need, in each parish, to establish support groups to nourish those whose lives have come undone.

Preventing divorce. There are few, if any, surefire methods of preventing divorce. But certainly a couple's attitudes toward marriage need to be carefully developed before any wedding takes place. Beyond romance, passion and the big wedding lies the real world. And engaged couples need to ask themselves: am I entering marriage for the long distance, or am I really only "giving it a try"?

The glue. I am blessed to work in a program called Retrouvaille (Rediscovery). It is a weekend and follow-up experience for couples in marital crisis. It has been very successful in healing marriages that seemed to be over. Retrouvaille contains no miracle cure, no "quick fix." It simply teaches couples the fundamentals of effective communication, forgiveness and love. It impacts not only on marital discord but on the basic problems facing families in America today. The glue for healing our wounded families is the same principle we try to use in Respect Life programs. All life has its source in God. God gives life. All life is ultimately returning to God. Our beginning and our end is God. That fact makes life, and wives, and husbands, and children, and families sacred. If we really believe in the holiness of each created person our families would be in much healthier shape. But so long as the sacred is what we do in church, and not what we live at home, our families will continue to suffer without hope.

(If you would like more information on the state of the American family and how we can respond to the problems of Christian family life, you might want to secure a copy of the document, *A Family Perspective in Church and Society.* Write to United States Catholic Conference, 3211 4th St. N.E., Washington, D.C. 20017-1194)

Good Friends

Would you sacrifice $68,750 for a friend? Tony Eason did. He was a quarterback for the New England Patriots who was traded to the New York Jets. He didn't like that idea. Not because he didn't care for the Jets, but because he'd be in competition with fellow quarterback Ken O'Brien, a treasured friend with whom he grew up. And Tony Eason thought that good friends shouldn't compete for the same job. So, he sat out his contract and it cost him $68,750 as a penalty. Finally, with encouragement from O'Brien, he decided to join the team. The whole situation was well summarized by Leigh Steinberg, an agent who represents the two football players: "Ken O'Brien is one of Tony Eason's closest and most cherished friends. His feeling is that friendship is more important than money."

A story like this makes you wonder: what is the meaning of friendship, and how far would you go for a friend?

Experts who work with teenagers and young adults say that friendship is a deeply desired value. Most young people want friends very badly. And yet, friendship is equally often betrayed. Wonder why? Well, it seems that our ideals don't match our real-life actions when it comes to friendship. And in determining how good we are at establishing and maintaining friendships, we need to look at several issues:

1. What are we looking for in a friend? Most friendships just happen. And that's good in being a sign of spontaneity, but bad if we don't ask ourselves, "Is this person someone who's good for me?" We will be, throughout our lives, attracted to any number of people and things which really aren't in our best interest. There's nothing wrong with making a "friend assessment" before we commit to another person.

2. Is this a reciprocal relationship? That means, is it going both ways? I should be happy to do what I can to help my friends. But there's nothing wrong with letting them do for me too. A one-way friendship can be frustrating. There should be give and take on *both* sides.

3. Am I a fickle friend? Some people aren't very deep. They'll love you when you look good, have money, have a car, or are popular. But lose any of these "attractions" and you're history.

Friends shouldn't just be had to see what we can get from them. That's using people, and using people is wrong.

4. Do I ever tell my friends good things about them? Some people find it very hard to praise a friend. It's as if we're afraid of being really nice. There's nothing wrong with affirmation and praise. It helps my friend to appreciate himself more, and it lets him know that I care about his goodness.

5. Is having fun the best test for friendship? Many friends will offer us the best of times. But there may be a long-range price to pay for the "fun." So a friend who promotes drugs, alcohol, smoking, easy sex or any other negative action is really not a "good" friend. If I lead my friend down a destructive path, I'm really a lousy friend.

6. Am I a trustworthy friend? We all want to be able to tell our friends the inner workings of our hearts. But it hurts like heck to hear our confidences bounced around by an unfaithful friend. Gossip destroys trust. If your friend entrusts you with a secret, be worthy of the confidence. Keep your mouth zipped.

7. Are we longing for friendship far and wide, when it's right in front of us all the time? Many of my friends in high school and college are hoping to find a really "best friend." They'll search forever to find someone to trust, to love, to talk with and to listen. But, sometimes we're looking too hard. The friend is right in front of us. That friend may well be our own parents, our own brothers, our own sisters.

In the movie *Steel Magnolias*, the daughter (played by Julia Roberts) is battling constantly with her mom (played by Sally Fields). But long past the little wars, they both share a love which no one else can touch. They truly are best friends. They don't have to look any further than their own home to find the awesome gift of friendship.

Getting Off the Ride

I hate being trapped. And I remember a ride at the Rye Beach amusement park that always made me feel trapped. It was called "the Steeplechase," and it moved with what seemed to me as a kid to be incredible speed. Once you got on it, there was no getting off. If you tried to break away in the middle of the ride, you'd be a goner. It was like being at the top of the first huge hill on the roller coaster, and wondering why you ever got on the stupid ride, and knowing that there is no exit now. The only way out is down.

I ran into my high school classmate, Dave, recently. He was someone we "partied" with. We all move through the partying experiences of life. Dave did not. Alcohol and drugs were for him a ride he couldn't get off.

We all presume, I think, that experimenting is something we all go through. We believe that we will have our good times and then move on. As a priest, though, I've seen another side of partying. I stay in touch with a lot of my high school classmates. I celebrate their weddings, baptize their children and bury their loved ones. And staying in touch has allowed me to see that many friends, like Dave, never moved past the alcohol, the drugs, the partying. Their development as people is arrested during high school, they get trapped and hooked on ways of living that permanently alter their future.

In most cases they did not get "hooked" all by themselves. They were introduced to their poison by people they called "friends." But the truth is that anyone who promotes the need for me to alter my state of consciousness (read: getting high) in order to find happiness is a liar. Such people are really a bed of quicksand posing as friends.

Because, you see, we really don't know who of our friends can, and who can't, handle drugs and alcohol, so that when I push the partying scene it's really not unlike promoting a game of Russian roulette. Somebody will be hurt, and hurt badly. I am sure that my high school friends thought that Dave, like the rest of us, could party and then move on with his life. But he didn't. He couldn't. And we, who encouraged him to party, were really placing Dave over a trap door that would inevitably collapse. And collapse it did.

His drinking and drugging made college impossible; he dropped out after a semester. He has never been able to keep a job. He never really developed skills for a career. His interpersonal relationships all self-destructed. I know that Dave often gives way to despair. He's attempted suicide.

And when I see Dave I always want to cry. We were there at the beginning. We could have been a way out if we'd only recognized the signs. But we didn't or couldn't. We presumed that he was just like us, and he isn't. And, in moments of intense honesty, we have to face our responsibility. We all helped to joyride our friend down a road of self-destruction. We just never considered the consequences of our partying. True friends do.

True friends are sensitive to the effects their actions have on those they care for. We should have noticed that Dave needed to party too much. We should have seen that for him, partying wasn't a lark, it was a necessity. And when he was in need of money for drugs or alcohol, we should have had the courage to say no. Not to supply him.

For Dave and for perhaps as many as 20 to 30 percent of our friends, drugs and alcohol are the "Steeplechase," the ride they just can't get off. Real friends do all they can to keep those we love from ever getting on that ride toward no exit.

Remembering Michael

Michael was my cousin. We were born a year apart. And as I have two sisters, he was — for a time — like a brother to me. Being a year older made him feel protective of me. We lived in Brooklyn, and Michael was an intuitive street kid. He had smarts about real life I couldn't even begin to have. Michael was cool. He knew the deal. I admired him. He was also talented. Not in an academic way, but with an ability to read people. He was sensitive; he was funny; he could be very kind; he was handsome; and he was charming. He could get you to believe that whatever he said was the absolute truth. Even if it was all bull.

Somewhere, during high school I think, Michael and I started to head down different roads. He got involved with a world that was foreign to me. He drank a lot; he did drugs a lot; he fooled around a lot. And sometimes he got burnt.

His parents, his teachers and some of his friends would try to challenge him to pull it all together. But he was an unbelievable con-man. He would look you in the eyes; tell you that drugs and alcohol were the worst; swear he was finished with them; get you to smile supportively; and be stoned the next day.

This went on for years. And the truth is that we all knew that he was full of it. We wanted to believe in him enough that we accepted what we should have rejected. I can remember many occasions when I'd be sitting with Mike and asking him about how his "problem" was coming. And he would, as always, assure me that things had been low, but now he was really on the right track. One time, to confirm the ruse, he even gave me some of the pills he'd been addicted to. "Throw them out," he said. "I wanna be clean again." I bought the act only to find out that what he'd given me was only a fraction of what he had. And, you know, deep down I always knew he was lying. But it's so hard to say that. It's so difficult to look at someone you love, listen to their stories and to blow them out of the water by telling them that you're not buying a word of it. Maybe sometimes I wanted to keep Michael's love and friendship more than I needed to expose the unspoken truth.

One day, a few years ago, the lies caught up with Michael. He got up in the middle of the night and took into his body more than it could handle. He overdosed, and died within hours.

His death devastated us all. We should have seen it coming, but I guess we denied the inevitable. Our feelings during the wake and funeral were all jumbled. We were angry about drugs; we were angry with Michael; we were angry with God; and if we were really honest, we'd have to admit we were most angry with ourselves. Because, deep down, we knew that we could have done more.

During the Christmas season our families get together to celebrate a lot of wonderful values. But sometimes the holidays also give us opportunities we miss. We've got a chance to be with the people we love. Partying with them, eating with them, going to church with them, giving gifts to them, are all important and good; but we also need to use our times together to tell each other the truth. Even truths that made us uncomfortable or angry.

For some strange reason, the holidays reawaken our memories. And my memories are often of Michael. I miss him. I loved him, and I wish I had loved him enough to say "stop."

Whatever the person you love is doing — drugs, drinking, sex, lying, cheating, stealing, or putting people down — it's a true sign of caring to confront and to challenge. Real friends aren't the ones who tell us "yes, yes, yes." Our truest friends may have to say no. And "no" is, after all, a love word too.

Going to Church

I was heading over to church one Sunday morning to help with Communion. When I got to the sacristy, I realized that the priest celebrating Mass was just completing his homily. So I decided to take a walk outside and catch some of the terrific weather we were enjoying.

As I shot out a side door I bumped into two sheepish teenage guys who were obviously into "cutting out." They clutched in their hands copies of the parish bulletin: parental notification of the fact that they had "been to Mass." "Busy day?" I asked them. "No," said the honest older boy, "we're just bored."

This all took me back to the memory of a friendship I've enjoyed for over 17 years. One of my closest friends is a fellow named Joe Lukaszewski. Recently we were considering the elements that have kept us good friends over all these years. It isn't excitement: sometimes we bore each other. It isn't intellectual: sometimes our conversation is dull beyond belief. It isn't the richness of our personalities: we both can be annoying, obnoxious and difficult to be around. It isn't power or money: we haven't got any. In fact, it's not friendship based on anything more than our desire to be loyal, to be committed, and to be there for each other. It's less a "feeling" of friendship than a commitment to a decision to be friends.

And friendship, I think, is at the heart of our God-life, too. Sometimes going to church can be boring, dull and intellectually vacant. And if we're going to Mass expecting an exciting floor show, we'll surely be disappointed. Rather, we're there because our friend Jesus has invited us to be there. If we're true friends, we'll take that invitation seriously. That means we'll face and reject all the nonsense we use as excuses for staying away, like:

"I'm really busy." There are 168 hours in every week. We somehow find the time to eat, to sleep, to go to school, to play sports, to be with people we care about, to fool around and to hang out. In fact, we find or make the time for anything we really believe is important. If our friend Jesus and his people are important, we'll make the time to be there.

"But the homilies are so boring." Give me a break. If we switched off everyone and everything that's boring in life, we'd all stay home in bed. The priest is trying. He may not be great, but at least he's giving it his best. Shouldn't we try to listen? And more to the point: we're not just there for the homily. We go to be part of a community who need us and miss us when we're absent. We go to receive the Body of Christ, who never bores us (or gives up on us).

"Look, I can find God in many places, I don't need a church building to pray." That's true. But let's be honest: if you don't go to church, how much serious praying do you really do? And further, where (outside of church) can you go to receive Communion? Are they giving it out someplace else? More importantly, Jesus told us in no uncertain terms: I want you to gather with other believers to celebrate my life. That means church.

"I used to go, but I had a really bad experience at church." We have all had some bad experience of church. But again, let's compare our experience of God's friendship with the rest of our lives. If every time you had a poor experience with your mother, your father, your sister, your brother, your friends, you said, "That's it, this relationship's over," we'd have no relationships at all. But we keep at relationships that matter. We forgive, we compromise and we try to love again. Any relationship worth having is worth working on. Why not give the same energy to our love of God and his church as we give to our friends and family?

Our Inconvenient Savior

Back when I was on my high school debate team, we were instructed by our astute coach to be on the lookout for that moment when our opponents would throw away reason and go for the emotional "punch." What they couldn't score with logic they'd replace with heartstring manipulation. Sometimes they could be very convincing. It was our task to remind the judges gently but firmly that as moving as our opposition sounded, they were full of it!

Oftentimes I'm required to debate again, only the issues are more serious now: they are matters of life and death. And once again there exists that key moment when our Planned Parenthood friends and their co-conspirators in the death industry go for the emotional "punch." Failing to convince us that the unborn child isn't really a human person, and ignoring their own 1960s handbook which read, "An abortion kills the life of a baby after it has begun. It is dangerous to your life and health. It may make you sterile so that when you want a child you cannot have it," they use their trump card. They argue that we need legal abortion if only to deal with the many cases of rape or incest, or to eliminate physical danger for an expectant mother, or (they rhetorically ask) how can we ask a woman to carry a child who may be born handicapped? The arguments sound neat and convincing. They really are terribly clever. They play off most people's worst fears for their loved ones. But, you see, they also always leave out the clarifying facts about their "worst case scenarios." They omit, for example, the figures. Of the almost two million abortions performed each year in our nation, fewer than two percent have anything to do with rape, incest, danger to the life of the mother or the possibility of a handicapped child being born. Nor do they ever attempt to address the fundamental question of these crisis pregnancies: does the way in which a child is conceived make the child any less innocent or worthy of the opportunity to be born?

Putting aside the two percent that touch on traumatic considerations, how do we explain the motive behind the other 98 percent of the abortions which occur each year in America? Could it be that the children are inconvenient? These children are "in the way," not part of the plans we make for our lives, guilty of poor timing in arriving on the human scene.

Decisions of convenience. Think about it. Aren't we, all of us, inconvenient and burdensome for others at sometime in our lives? Once we accept the premise that an unborn child can be eliminated because it is inconvenient, we really diminish all of our lives. Think of the elderly: they too can be in the way, they cost a lot to keep healthy and alive, and they're an awful drain on the energies of their younger caretakers. Think of the handicapped and disabled: they certainly never can contribute to our world the way we do, they need special care and consideration, they make us uncomfortable and uneasy because they're "different." Think of the terminally ill: they're going to die anyway and their medical bills can be so high — why not eliminate the problem before it gets out of hand? Let's pull the plug early and save ourselves the needless worry and mess later. Think of the poorest of the poor, the street people, they too are "in the way," they're a frightening sight and they serve no "useful" purpose in society. Why not put them permanently out of our field of vision?

We are *all*, at times, a source of inconvenience for others. We will *all*, at times, be a burden for others to carry. And yet, isn't that really part of what being fully human is all about? Isn't being with and for one another tenderly and compassionately, in the good times and the not so good times, part and parcel of the human and Christian vocation?

Each December we celebrate the birth of perhaps the most inconvenient child ever conceived: Jesus, the Lord. His mother, Scripture scholars say, was probably about 16 when she conceived him. She had no visible means of support: no job, little education. The fellow she was engaged to was not the father of the child. The law of the land said that if you conceive a child out of wedlock, the people of the town should take you to the outskirts of the village and stone you to death. If anyone had a right to argue that her pregnancy was "inconvenient" it was Mary, the mother of Jesus. And yet can you imagine how different all of our lives would be had Mary said no instead of yes?

Our God is a God of life and hope and possibility. He is a God who enjoins us to lift and carry the burdens and inconveniences of life with gratitude for the chance to care lovingly for the weakest. The world sometimes seems more inclined to celebrate a god called convenience. To such a god, especially at Christmas, we respond: "Bah! Humbug!"

On Being "Perfect"

I ran into Meg recently, a woman who was a dear friend of my oldest sister. They went through grammar school and high school together. Meg was, for a time, a regular fixture around our home. Now 37, she shared with me the happy news of an awaited child. She is seven months pregnant.

Meg also told me something that I found disturbing. She said she had not told her family about the pregnancy until the fourth month. That sounded strange to me. She explained, as if reading the concern in my face, that she wanted to have the amniocentesis test performed first. She wanted to be sure that her expected child would be "perfect."

I could not help wondering, when I left Meg, what she would have done had the test results indicated that her baby was less than perfect. Most people who undergo the amniocentesis test respond to the news of a possibility that the child will be born with a handicap or disability by aborting their unborn child. If my baby is not perfect, they reason, isn't it really better to eliminate it now and save everyone the pain later on? Better for whom? Certainly not the child whose life is ended.

Thinking through the popular idea which claims that the only valuable life is the life we deem "perfect" reminds me of my friend Paul O'Sullivan. Paul O'Sullivan was a teenager with Down's syndrome whom I knew and loved in my first parish assignment. I was the moderator of the altar boys and Paul was one of the best. Conscientious and dependable, Paul was a model of devotion. In the ways of the world, Paul really could not do much: his handicap made success, as the world measures it, an unattainable goal. But Paul could love, and he did that better than anyone I have ever known. You see, in his disability, Paul O'Sullivan was never able to develop the defenses and the manipulations we all create to measure and guard our affections. He simply loved freely and constantly. He hugged and he kissed and did not care who saw it. He could say that he loved others without embarrassment. His "handicap," his "limit" left him unlimited in the only power that matters in our world, the power to love another human being.

In his late teens Paul developed serious heart problems. These illnesses became progressively worse, and one day Paul O'Sullivan died. As a parish priest I had officiated at several hundred funerals. It was the unusual person who had present more than fifty or sixty friends and relatives at a funeral. Some really "big" people might have a few hundred at their funeral. But when Paul died it was different. The kid who loved others packed the place. People who had more intelligence than Paul, people with more important positions in life, people with more money, all came to say good-bye and pay their respects to a man who was handicapped. All seemed to realize that this had been a special child of God.

I hope and pray that people like my friend Meg have healthy babies. But I also hope she and others know that life is sacred and beautiful for those whom the world sees as less than perfect too.

As St. Paul writes in his letter to the Corinthians, "God purposely chose what the world considers foolish in order to put wise men to shame, and what the world considers weak in order to put the powerful to shame. He chose what the world looks down on, and despises, and thinks nothing of, in order to humble what the world believes is important" (1 Cor 1:27-28). Rest well, dear and loving Paul. To me you were and are perfect.

Father Gerry and Susan

How many of us remember the homily we heard in church last weekend? Most of us are lucky if we can recall the priest's or deacon's words by the end of Sunday night. There are many reasons for that situation. Sometimes we don't listen well. Sometimes we're distracted in church. Sometimes the preacher is boring, unprepared or repetitive. Sometimes his message is dull or lacking in any contemporary connection. There are many reasons for our weak memories when it comes to the recollection we have or don't have of the homilies we hear.

Let me tell you about a homily I heard over twenty years ago: I remember it to this day. It was delivered by a priest named Gerald J. Ryan. He was serving our diocese as director of Catholic Charities. He was a man of enormous compassion and insight. His words were so powerfully reflective of the logical marriage of the human and the divine, that they've echoed in my heart and mind for over two decades.

Msgr. Ryan began by telling us about a phone call he received when he was first ordained. A young couple whom he knew had just given birth to their first child and were devastated by the knowledge that their first-born was delivered without legs. The baby, a little girl, was weak and plagued with a number of life-threatening diseases. The doctors gave an unpromising prognosis.

The baby, the parents were told, would probably not make it. Some physicians advised the couple to do "very little" for the child, and allow it to die. The alternatives, they warned, were frightening. The parents were told that they would face a lifetime of misery if the child survived. Father Gerry spent considerable time with this hurting young couple. He helped them to see that they had planned to love their baby completely before she was born. And now that she was here, they should continue to love her with the same love they had originally intended. That was a hard message to swallow.

In their mind's eye, these good people had been expecting a beautiful and perfect child. They had, instead, gotten a child without legs and burdened with a host of related infirmities. Their hopes were dashed every time they looked into the bassinet at their woeful little daughter. But they did not give in. They stuck by their child. It was tough, very tough.

Where other children delighted their parents with the ability to walk, little Susan could only crawl. Where most parents visited pediatricians once or twice every few months, Susan was a weekly visitor to costly specialists. Her parents tried (sometimes failing, sometimes succeeding) to love her as she was, ignoring the difference and accepting her as normal, as God had created her.

Msgr. Ryan took us through each step of Susan's life. He did not sugar-coat the struggle and the pain. His homily ended with an experience he shared with Susan's family the week before his homily. It ended on the stage of American University, where Susan proudly moved across the stage to accept her college diploma. She would move next to medical school. At that graduation, tear-stained but elated, sat Susan's parents. Their treasured child, unwhole in the eyes of so many the day she was born, was more complete than most of us could ever hope to be.

Msgr. Ryan returned to his seat. The church was silent. Moments later it exploded in applause, as we came to realize that Susan was, with her parents, bringing forward the gifts of bread and wine.

That day at Mass taught me so much. It showed me that what we consider "wholeness" is sometimes so incomplete, and that in the wonder of God's plan, crazy as it sometimes seems, he does know what he's doing. Today, when I remember that homily some twenty years later, I'm also reminded of the power priests and deacons have to touch us and challenge us profoundly about the sacredness of life. Father Ryan, Monsignor Ryan, who became Bishop Gerald Ryan, is gone now, but his tender message remains.

Requiescat in pace to the priest who gave hope on that night of despair to Susan's mom and dad. May all of us have the fortitude to do the same.

Foolish Feminism

Sister Marjorie McGregor is a classic liberal. She cares about the poor; thinks we build too many bombs; feels we should interfere less in Central America; gets angry about the sexism she perceives in the Church; detests apartheid; uses terms like "collaborative ministry"; opposes the death penalty; and believes in national health care and a host of other progressive programs. So, imagine my surprise when I found her sitting on the ground next to me waiting to be arrested at a New York City abortion clinic.

Marjorie was one of a thousand people joining in non-violent civil disobedience, a now well-known national effort called Operation Rescue. And the sight of this sensitive, liberal woman being carried away on a police stretcher was really not so surprising.

You see, Marjorie believes that any true liberal must care about the weak, the innocent, the defenseless. And in her mind, that certainly includes the pre-born child.

Marjorie McGregor identifies herself as a pro-life feminist. Now, that will anger other feminists who have decided that pro-lifer and feminist are contradictory terms. They are not. In fact, in light of recent revelations, any feminist who is not working to save unborn children is not a feminist, but an oppressor.

Consider these stories. In recent news stories both the liberal *New York Times* and the *National Catholic Reporter* have featured front-page stories on abortion selection. It seems that in both the Third World and our country modern technology is allowing parents to know what sex their expected baby will be. And once that information is discovered, people are choosing to have abortions if the baby isn't the sex they want. And (listen up, "pro-choice" feminist) the vast majority of abortions are being performed on female unborn children.

In India, for example, a survey of 8,000 abortions performed in Bombay revealed that 7,999 were female pre-born babies. Once the parents of these unborn realized that they were carrying a little girl and not a "more desirable" son, they disposed of the child immediately.

74

And that happens not only in India. Studies show that in China, the Soviet Union, England, and in the United States, if prenatal testing reveals the presence of a female fetus, her chances of being eradicated are 65 percent better than a little boy's.

So, when a woman claims to be a feminist and supports abortion, she is truly living a violent contradiction. The pro-choice feminist is working for the destruction of her own sex.

Add in these factors: until recently, the only way to determine the baby's sex was through the test called amniocentesis. That test is conducted in the second trimester of pregnancy. A mother would be given the information during her fourth, fifth or sixth month of pregnancy.

That means we can view sex selection abortion as both an act of sexism and of barbarism. We are destroying children in the second trimester of pregnancy because we don't like their sex.

And doctors can't walk away without real responsibility for these violent events. *The New York Times* reports that over 20 percent of geneticists support abortion based on sex selection. They quote a Dr. Michael A. Roth, an obstetrician from Detroit, on the issue: "I have no ethical problems with it (abortion for sex selection), absolutely not. I think that abortion should be available on demand. I haven't turned anybody down."

Watch out, little girls, Dr. Roth and his like are out there willing to "assist" any woman in her "right" to choose to destroy any baby they select. And, lately, a lot more girl babies are ending up on the M.T.P. list (a wonderful euphemism for abortion; it stands for medical termination of pregnancy).

As we waited for the police to take us to be booked in New York, Sister Marjorie looked around the large crowd. And then with a look of regret she said, "God, I wish there were more true feminists involved in this cause." And from where I sit, Marjorie is right on target.

What true feminist can rest comfortably with the knowledge that women are dying each day just because they are little girls and not little boys?

In the stomach-churning climactic scene of the movie *Sophie's Choice*, Meryl Streep enters a holocaust death camp. There she is challenged by a Nazi to give up either her son or her daughter for elimination. She painfully gives her daughter over to death. She never knows peace again. Sophie's choice continues to be made in our time.

Seamless Garment: Dirty Words?

In the conflict that occurred between the Vatican and the pro-choice Sisters who signed a *New York Times* ad which affirmed a right to abort, a compromise was suggested. The seeming impasse between the pro-choice signers and the pro-life Vatican negotiators could be ended if the Sisters would affirm the "sacredness" or "sanctity" of all life, especially the unborn. In a strange and difficult response, two of the Sisters said no. They would not use those words because, they said, they were the language of "the enemy." Not much room for dialogue here.

Are the words "sacredness" or "sanctity" simply political words invented by Vatican officials, or do they reflect a truth as deep as God? When the Church calls human life sacred, it is saying that because of life's origin. The source of our creation is God. That's not my opinion or Pope John Paul's. It's biblical. In Psalm 139 we read, "It was you who created my inmost self and put me together in my mother's womb. You know me through and through, for having watched my bones take shape when I was being formed in secret, knitted together in the limbo of the womb."

Our sacredness is further affirmed by our final destination: heaven. We begin with God and he is our final resting place. That makes us sharers in the divine.

Further, unlike any other creatures on the planet, Scripture confirms that we are "made in the image and likeness of God." We are his children, his handiwork. If we believe that human life is holy, then we must believe that all life is sacred, because all life is begun by God.

That means that the unborn baby is sacred life, but so is the handicapped, the elderly, the AIDS patient, the street person, the convict on death row, the drug abuser, the drug pusher, the prostitute, the communist, the person of another religion, the person of another color, the semi-comatose aunt who lives on a feeding tube. It means every man, woman and child, born and unborn. If we're made in the image and likeness of God, then his

76

image is multifaceted and we are to love and treasure every side of God's incredible face.

That message, the sacredness of every life, is a hard one to own. The 1988 presidential debates proved that. On the Democrat side we had a man who would fight like the dickens for the life of a convict, but ignore the killing of unborn children.

The flip side of the contradiction was reflected in the Republican candidate. He believes that unborn children are sacred but will back death for the convict.

They both miss the point.

If the convicted murderer has a right to life, then so must the unborn child. And if that unborn baby is sacred, it is sacred because of its connection to the Creator. And that same Creator created the convict.

Living out a consistent ethic of life isn't easy. It's much easier to claim that some lives are more valuable than others. But once we accept qualifiers like that, we set ourselves up for the same tragic equivocation promoted by the pro-choice lobby.

There was a time, years ago, when the pro-abortionists would argue that a fetus wasn't really a person. It was just a "mass of tissue" in a woman's body. But medical science and fetology have put the lie to that ruse.

No person with brains is denying the personhood of the in-utero child anymore. I attended a talk recently given by a director of Planned Parenthood (the biggest aborters in America). The woman speaking surprised me. Rather than denying the personhood of the unborn baby, she admitted it. But, she said, while a fetus is a baby, a person, a human being, it has less value than a grown woman, because the mother has more "life experience." Another incredible equivocation!

And therein lies the danger of ignoring a consistent ethic of life. The pro-abortionists put qualifiers on life, some have value, some do not. Now, if pro-lifers accept that some life (namely the unborn) has value, while other life (the convicted murderer, for example) has no value well then, we're really playing in the same ballpark as the compromisers of life.

Let's do it God's way. He made us all, the good and the less good, the beautiful and the ugly, the innocent and those who choose sin, the well and the sick. Let's let him be the judge of value, and let us praise and celebrate all his human handiwork.

What We Really Believe

One night I found myself rolling through the zillion and one cable stations on television looking for something worthwhile to watch. I came upon an interview program, and the guest was mega-entrepreneur Ted Turner. Now, you've got to, at least, admire the man's business acumen, if not his sensitivity or compassion. He was asked about his stand on abortion. He had no problem with it at all, he said. He then explained why. People, he reasoned, have miscarriages all the time, "and no one makes a fuss over that." So, he figured, abortion is just kind of a "planned miscarriage." What, he wondered, was all the commotion about? Obviously Ted Turner never spent any quality time with a mother-to-be who has miscarried. If he did, he'd know that those who miscarry or deliver stillborn babies go through a very real sense of loss and grief. It is a true experience of bereavement, and the pain is real. In fact, support groups are springing up around the country for this kind of bereavement (called perinatal grief).

Ted Turner wasn't connected to the sense of new life which begins at conception. And when that new life is interrupted in its development, whether through abortion or miscarriage, a sense of emptiness can consume the expectant parents. And that's because we expect a new baby with each pregnancy. Not a fetus, a baby. Who of us has ever walked up to a pregnant woman and asked her, "How's your fetus doing?" We ask her about "the baby," because that's what it is. Or, have you ever gone to a "fetus shower"? No, you go to celebrate life by attending a baby shower.

Recently I saw again how easy it is for us all to lose a sense of life's importance from the moment of conception. Very dear friends, Susan and Tom, were happily expecting their first child. One day, for no understandable reason, their baby simply died. It was somewhere between the third and fourth month of pregnancy. At the hospital Susan asked her doctor to preserve the baby intact. Her doctor suggested evacuating the baby with a suction machine, the same tool used for abortion. Susan insisted that another way to bring forth her small child be found. Her doctor's first suggestion upset and troubled her.

Susan's husband, Tom, then called their parish church to arrange a funeral. The priest that answered told them that funerals aren't necessary for children who die in the womb before the sixth month. And Tom accepted this, realizing that his baby was already with God and so didn't necessarily need a funeral Mass. Susan, however, saw it differently. "Well," she said, "let's at least have a memorial Mass for our own spiritual enrichment." Back Tom went to the phone. He got a different priest who again squashed the idea of a Mass. His reasons centered around the earliness of the pregnancy. And then he said the unfortunate words I'm sure he must regret: "If we had to do a Mass for every miscarried or stillborn baby, we'd be doing Masses till we're ready to drop."

Now, while I understand this priest's anxiety about the proliferation of Masses (a very genuine concern), the message he sent to Susan and Tom was, nonetheless, damaging. They read it as: "It isn't a real baby yet, so what's all the fuss and bother about?"

I caught Susan on the upswing and she let me have it good: "You know, Father Jim, you folks in the Church are real quick to say that from the moment of conception it is a baby, a person, a unique creation. But when it comes to backing your words with consolation in times of miscarriage, you sure don't act like you believe that we lost a child, a baby whom we love."

Miscarriage and stillbirth involve the loss of real people, whom we looked to celebrate in life, too sadly taken from us through confusingly swift death. A true respect for all human life means that the Susans and Toms will find in our Church a deep sense of empathy for their grief and their loss. If we don't offer that to the good people who suffer from the loss of their children, then we're not a whole lot smarter or more sensitive than the Ted Turners of our society.

Parental Consent

I had dinner recently with a terrific young couple named John and Lois Donnelly. And before we sat down to eat we spent some time with their children, Lauren and Steven. They are a beautiful family, and they work hard to build this loving community.

I remember when they were considering a new home that John and Lois were really concerned about the needs of their children above all. They investigated the school district they would attend to be sure that it offered quality education. They examined the neighborhood carefully to be sure that their children would meet a wide variety of people. They made sure that the commute to and from work was reasonable so that John could be home early enough to truly enjoy his children and share fully in the responsibility of raising them with Lois. And like many young couples, John and Lois try to create a healthy home for their offspring. They avoid fats, sugars and salt. They exercise and try to stay in shape. They are also very safety conscious and want their home to be a place the children can live in without fear.

Even on a spiritual level John and Lois live out a real concern for their children's welfare. Like many couples they had put church on a back burner after their wedding. But as the children started to arrive, they felt a need to bring a more formal spiritual formation into their lives. They seemed to recognize that the love of God and the support of a faith community could only further enhance their lives. And so, at least initially for their children's sake, they moved back to the Church.

John and Lois are not atypical. Many parents direct their lives and their energies toward the welfare of their children. They move in selfless and giving directions, which radically change their lives. They do it because of the love they feel for this precious gift from God: their children.

Consider now this reality. John and Lois love, nurture, feed, clothe, encourage, counsel, give medical care to and shelter their children. Throughout their children's growth they are consulted and advised. Their permission is sought on every major decision affecting their children by school and society. No doctor will pull a tooth without parental permission. No teacher will take their daughter on a school field trip without parental consent. No nurse will dispense an aspirin without checking with the parents. No store will pierce a child's ear without receiving parental authorization. And these facts all highlight an important parental right: the right to know what is happening in the life of the child they love. Even the Supreme Court recognized the importance of this respect for parents when in 1979 it proclaimed:

"Minors often lack the experience, perspective and judgment to recognize and avoid choices that could be detrimental to them. Parents are *entitled* to the support of laws designed to aid the discharge of their parental responsibility."

Why then, we might ask, is abortion the one decision about which parents presently have no rights at all? A minor, say age 15, finds out she is pregnant (over one million teenagers become pregnant every year in America). As the law presently stands, she can go to her teacher; get pro-abortion counseling; be driven to an abortion clinic; have her baby destroyed; in some places have the abortion paid for by the state; and then return home to parents who know nothing of what has transpired.

Oh, there is one catch! If the teenager develops post-abortion complications (and there are plenty of possibilities, like a perforated uterus, a uterine infection, major hemorrhaging, high fever or emotional trauma), then the responsibility for that teenager reverts back to her parents. If the girl is "broken" physically or emotionally by her abortion experience, that's her parents' problem. The same folks who were shut out of the decision to abort are then legally obligated to "pick up the pieces of their child's life."

Pro-abortion spokespersons will often use polls to support the right of people to abort freely. But polls do not help them on the parental consent issue. In the 1983 national Garth poll some 71 percent of the American population believed that parents should be involved in a decision which so profoundly affects their children.

During the early 1960s we would hear awful stories of communist totalitarian antics wherein parents and their children would be encouraged to betray each other. Parents who were unfaithful to the party line could be arrested if their children "fingered them." We all recoiled at that image because we believed that the state simply has no right to come between parents and their children. And yet, presently on abortion, the state is separating parents and their children at what must be seen as one of the most crucial decisions anyone can make: to give life or to take it.

I really admire John and Lois. They are doing everything a parent can to raise healthy and loving children. I hope and pray that they will always be allowed to share a part of each and all of the major moments in their children's lives. How tragic it would be if laws, which supposedly protect "privacy," acted only to separate a child from the best friends she has in this world: devoted parents.

School-Based Health Clinics: No Answer At All

Many of my teenage friends smoke cigarettes. No one who really cares about them encourages their continued use. Many of my teenage friends drink heavily and "party" using drugs that can seriously damage. No one who loves them would ever encourage their continued use. In fact, were we to respond to smoking, drinking or drugging by saying, "Well, they're going to do it anyway, so we might as well cooperate with them," we'd be irresponsible at best and morally reprehensible at worst. No, if we see young people we care about heading down a messed-up path, love compels us to discourage taking that route. We are compelled to encourage positive alternatives. And therein lies the problem with the rise of school-based health clinics. They exist to encourage and promote a pattern of life which is severely detrimental to the self-image and general welfare of our young people.

These clinics have been pushed on us recently in response to the so-called "epidemic" of teen sexual activity. Every major television network and national magazine has trumpeted this notion of widespread sexual acting out. This, in turn, gives legitimacy to the establishment of clinics which would exist to distribute birth control and make daily abortion referrals. In other words, the media's trying to sell us on reacting to this "crisis" by making contraception and abortion a down-the-school-hall easy-access option. Let's take a look at their rationale and see if it holds water.

A recent Louis Harris poll on teenage sexual activity tells us that teenagers who actually experience intercourse may be as low as 20 percent or as high as 32 percent. And while those percentages impact on many more teenagers than any of us would like to see, it does force us to realize that fully 68 percent of our teenagers are not engaging in intercourse. In other words, contrary to those who proclaim that we need sex health clinics in school because "everyone's doing it," the truth is, "everyone's" not.

83

And even for those who are, we must consider and examine the myriad negative factors school-based clinics will multiply. For example:

• The cost factor: School-based clinics will ultimately use our tax dollars. Each clinic will cost an estimated $250,000 to operate. That money will be supplied by the local school district budget. Which means that, once again, Catholic Christians will be legally compelled to pay for contraception and abortion even though both seriously violate our religious and moral beliefs.

• Clinics further erode our already badly damaged family systems. Clinics will allow a teenager to secure and use potentially damaging birth control (pills mostly) and secure abortion without parental notification or consent. In fact, the selling point of clinics is that students are given "complete confidentiality." Parents are expected to love, support, clothe, house, nurture and encourage their children but are not permitted to be a part of the most significant decisions a young person can make. We have here, clearly, a case of the state directly interfering in the special relationship between parent and child. If this sort of separation occurred in a totalitarian country, we'd swiftly condemn it. But it happens in our nation and is overlooked, considered to be a part of the price we must pay for so-called "reproductive freedom."

• Clinics promote greater sexual activity, not less. In a value-free environment where birth control and abortion are encouraged, teenagers have no reason to say no to sex. It's all okay, and there are (they come to believe) no lasting consequences. Without a reason to refrain, studies indicate, teenagers' sexual activity rate always increases. In school districts which have already established school-based clinics, intercourse increases by as much as 50 percent. Pregnancy rises and the number of abortions soar. Planned Parenthood tells us that school districts with clinics have a lower rate of live births. That's true. But they don't also tell us that the rate of births is down because the destruction of the unborn dramatically increases.

School-based clinics are clearly in no one's best interest. They increase the incidence of intercourse by creating the deception of an often-times faulty safety net called contraception. They ravage the already tenuous trust and communication between parent and child. They do not lead us to less pregnancy but more. And they increase the use of abortion as an escape clause for failed birth control. They in no way work to increase the sadly missing ingredient in teenage development: self-esteem.

School-based clinics will make some few people very rich. But for parents, their teenage children, the unborn, and our society, these clinics are the surest way to spiritual and moral impoverishment.

Informed Consent

When President Reagan announced his choice of Judge Robert H. Bork for the vacancy on our Supreme Court, many of us reacted with hope-filled joy. He might well have been the fifth pro-life justice we'd been hoping and praying for. But lest our joy be too pronounced, we had only to read the reaction of the pro-abortionists in the secular news media. Unable to challenge Judge Bork at the level of his legal scholarship or his personal integrity, the media, led by the strident Ted Kennedy, noted that Bork's "ideology" was unacceptable. They felt that only a "moderate" can replace Justice Lewis F. Powell. That "moderate" stuff can sound convincing unless you consider how a so-called moderate judge can assist in the destruction of some 22 million innocent unborn lives. Judge Powell was no moderate when it came to abortion. He not only voted with the majority in 1973 to legalize abortion at any time during the entire nine months of pregnancy, but he also saw to it that unlimited abortion was never impeded.

A classic example is the issue of informed consent. The law normally insists that every patient has a right to know how a particular surgery will affect him. Makes sense, no? And if a doctor doesn't tell you about the possible consequences of his surgical activity, he can be royally sued. Well, that law applies to every surgery, except abortion. In 1986, you see, the Supreme Court by a 5-4 vote said that you shouldn't tell a woman how an abortion will affect her. They felt that such information might "intimidate" her into choosing to give life. At issue was a law in the state of Pennsylvania. That state had been telling women about the physical and psychological risks of abortion. It was challenging people to think about what abortion really is. And as a priest, that sounds to me like a wise path to follow. If I've been told once, I've been told a hundred times by women who have had abortions, "Father, I just didn't know what it would all mean. No one told me about how I'd feel. No one warned me of the physical and emotional by-products of my abortion."

And what information should be a part of informed consent? There are several key facts that every person considering abortion should know:

1.   That there are some 7,000 *serious* complications from abortion.

2.   That both suction abortion and saline abortion are always painful for both the mother and her child.

3.   That there is always a risk of perforation of the uterus by the assorted instruments used by the aborting doctor.

4.   That this damaging laceration of the uterus can also be caused by the removal of the baby's bones and tissue.

5.   That the uterine perforation can cause ancillary damage to your bowels and bladder.

6.   That it is possible that the laceration will require a later hysterectomy.

7.   That the most common problem of even early abortion is infection from the pieces of the infant's tissue not completely eliminated by the doctor.

8.   That such infections can cause enough damage to your reproductive organs so that you may become sterile.

9.   That those who abort have a far greater chance of miscarriage when they later decide to carry their baby to term.

10.   That the unborn child's removal can cause severe convulsions and hemorrhaging.

11.   That since 1973 the maternal mortality rate for abortion after the fourth month is *higher* than childbirth. (And this fact has alarming significance when you realize that there are 125,000 late abortions, from the fourth to the ninth month, every year in America.)

12.   That severe depression, anxiety, suicidal tendency, sleeplessness and loss of self-image are *routine* emotional after-effects of abortion.

This is all heavy-duty information. The Court said that you shouldn't tell a woman this stuff, it might scare her out of having an abortion. Please God, it might!

All the News That Fits

Like most people, I believe what I read in the newspapers or see on the television news. That is, I used to. But recently, more and more, I notice that the media are spending less time *reporting* the news than they do *making* the news. And what they "make" is often just not true.

Now, I don't claim to have in-depth knowledge about every substantial issue facing our nation, but I do know a good deal about abortion and the right-to-life cause. And what I know, factually, is simply not what the media tell us. Often, and here I'd like to alter the masthead of *The New York Times,* they give us not "all the news that's fit to print," but "all the news that fits their point of view."

Some recent examples come to mind:

Item one: *The New York Times* summarizes their view of a Human Life Amendment: "In other words, given a choice between saving the fetus or the mother, the mother must die." That's not true. The Human Life Amendment takes several forms. The most likely amendment to be successful will include an exception clause to save the life of the mother.

More to the point, the *Times* is using a smoke-screen by sounding hysterical. They know full well that of the 1.7 million abortions performed in America annually, the surgeon general estimates that only a fraction of one percent of those involve abortions related to maternal risk. In other words most abortions have nothing to do with rape, incest, danger to the life of the mother or the possibility of a handicapped child being born.

Ninety-nine percent of the abortions in our country happen due to "social reasons" — the baby would not be convenient at this point in time. That fact comes to us from Dr. Irvin Cushner, U.S. deputy secretary for population affairs.

In other words, the *Times* is not only being melodramatic, but obscuring the truth.

Item two: *The Village Voice,* reporting on the pro-life platform of the Republican Party, tells us that right-to-lifers defend the life of the unborn while supporting the bombings of abortion clinics. They tell us that we believe killing is wrong "unless it involves blowing up abortion clinics." This kind of yellow journalism is particularly destructive to dialogue. The fact is that *every major pro-life organization* in America has firmly condemned clinic bombings.

Pro-lifers know that bombing is simply exchanging one form of violence for another. Crazy people, not pro-lifers, bomb clinics. You wouldn't know that to read *The Village Voice.*

Item three: *Cosmopolitan* carries an advice column which is apparently very popular with the trendy set. A woman recently wrote to the columnist, sounding obviously distraught over whether or not she should tell the man she loves that earlier in her life she had an abortion. Her guilt and pain over the abortion are evident in her letter.

Mrs. Irma Kurtz, the "expert" columnist, brushes off the very real feelings of remorse with superficial puff like, "I've had one (an abortion), for goodness sake, and can still smile at myself in a mirror." Ms. Kurtz then becomes a medical consultant as she writes, "There is not the least shred of evidence that a hygienic, efficient abortion should interfere in the slightest with your ability to have children in the future." Then our resident expert becomes a moralist as well: "Well, pregnancy is a possible side effect of making love; carelessness is not a sin. And if men could get pregnant, chances are he'd be the one telling you about his abortion."

How profound.

Irma Kurtz is not only uninformed but grossly insensitive. The fastest growing area of therapy in the country revolves around P.A.S., Post-Abortion Syndrome. Literally millions of women (and their boyfriends and husbands) deal daily with the awesome emotional and physical effects of abortion. The incidence of miscarriage among those who have had an abortion earlier in life is significant.

Doctor Bernard Nathanson estimates that there are at least 7,000 serious physical side effects from abortion each year. And, of course, you'll notice that Ms. Kurtz never bothers in her response to mention the baby, the primary victim of abortion. Like many media "scholars" she leaves out the innocent child, making the pre-born seem like an appendix instead of the human being he or she is.

None of these media manipulators will admit that while just under two million babies die each year through abortion, some two and a half million American couples long for a child to adopt. The media are untrue. They deal too often in half-truth. We need to keep that in mind every time we sit down to read or watch or listen to their "reporting."

Let me close with some "facts" about abortion you can believe in. They are the truth, a rare commodity in print these days.

Fact one: Approximately 1.7 million abortions are performed annually in our country. That's over 4,000 a day, one every 20 seconds. Government officials admit that these numbers are underestimated due to underreporting by physicians and medical facilities.

Fact two: The total number of Americans who have died in all the wars in which our country has fought since the Revolutionary War is less than the number of unborn children killed each year through abortion.

Fact three: Abortion became legal in 1973 when the United States Supreme Court ruled that pregnancy could be terminated at any time between conception and birth. Abortion is a nine-month right in our nation. Children born at five months, premature babies, live due to advances in medical technology.

Fact four: The fathers of unborn children have absolutely no say whatsoever in whether or not the child will live or be aborted. For while it takes two people to create a baby, and while a father will be legally bound to support the baby from the moment of birth through its 18th birthday, the dad has no rights and no say about the nine months his child spends in the womb.

Fact five: The first nation to legitimize the widespread use of abortion was the Soviet Union, followed by Nazi Germany, which encouraged abortion for Jews.

Fact six: The average abortion patient is between 15 and 24 years old, unmarried, white and childless. One-third of all abortion patients have had at least one previous abortion.

Of Polls and Persons

During most weekends of the year I visit different parishes to preach about the pro-life cause. I'd like to share one experience I had recently.

After the Saturday evening Mass ended most of those attending filed out through the rear door. I was there to shake hands with them, and they were exceedingly warm and affirming.

Suddenly, toward the end of the line, a woman appeared who looked incredibly angry. And as she passed me, instead of shaking my hand she slapped my face before exiting. I was, to say the least, deeply thrown by the experience. Throughout most of the night I wondered what I had said or done to upset her. I tried to imagine what I could have done that made even a modest dialogue impossible. I hoped and prayed that one day I might have the chance to see that young woman again.

God must have been listening. When I went down to celebrate the first Mass on Sunday morning she was there waiting for me in the sacristy. She greeted me with an accusation: "Because of you I didn't sleep at all last night." I responded, "Me either." I then told her that I was sorry that my homily on abortion had upset her.

She said that she needed to talk, and so we did. It seems that my speaking about abortion had reopened for her the memories of her own abortion seven years before. She had never resolved those feelings but had succeeded only in burying them, putting them aside to fester. Ultimately they had to come out.

She talked, and she cried, and she asked for the Lord's forgiveness. I also cried and was grateful for the opportunity to be an instrument of the Lord's unconditional forgiving love. Our meeting ended as she offered a warm hug and kiss, leaving with words of thanks. I rubbed my hand past the cheek which had taken the slap twelve hours earlier and pondered how far we'd come.

With the Pope's last visit to America many in the news media ran surveys of attitudes toward abortion. Not surprisingly for a news media which admits to being overwhelmingly pro-choice (82 percent say they favor current abortion laws), their questions were loaded and the results predictable. Their questions lacked distinctions.

They would always take one of two routes. They would either highlight the negative (e.g., "Do you favor a *ban* on *all* abortions?"), or lump all abortions in the same category ("Do you favor legalized abortion?").

They would, through their questions, try to eliminate an evaluation of the varieties of circumstances involved in pregnancy. In this way they would be able to highlight their "proof" that American Catholics disagree with their Pope in this incredibly important issue. Maybe Americans do, but I don't think so. Let's look at a more precise poll on the matter, one done by the Gallup organization in 1985. In that poll a broad base of Americans indicate that:

• Twenty-one percent favor unrestricted abortions.

• Twenty percent said all abortions should be illegal.

• Fifty-five percent said that there should be only limited abortions in special cases (e.g., rape, incest, danger to the life of the mother). This group also felt that abortion should be allowed in the first trimester only.

So if you add up those who oppose all abortion with those who want it severely limited, you come to 76 percent of people saying they want the current nine-month right to abortion changed. You certainly never heard those statistics from the national media during John Paul's visit.

And why, we need to ask, do so many people oppose unrestricted abortion? The answer is provided by yet another poll. Not long ago the *New York Times* and CBS News commissioned a poll which asked the fundamental question: "Is abortion murder?"

• Fifty-four percent of Americans said it was.

• Thirty-five percent said it was not.

The testimony of polls can inform us. But for me there is a deeper and more convincing reality. The eyes, the tears, the pain of the woman I met in that church taught me all I need to know. Abortion does destroy life, and there are always at least two victims: the baby and its mother, in whose memory the echo of life now gone remains forever.

NEW from Resurrection Press

THE HEALING OF THE RELIGIOUS LIFE

Robert Faricy, S.J. and Scholastica Blackborow
Foreword by George Maloney, S.J.

This book is meant neither for those religious who are
completely satisfied with the way the religious life is going,
nor for the complacent; nor is it for those who have lost all
hope. It is for those religious who know that the Lord is
faithful to his promises, that the Lord does not want their
religious institutes simply to go into oblivion...that he wants
to guide us to new and better things for the religious life and
for religious.

> "*The Healing of the Religious Life* is a book of hope –
> hope for the apparently dwindling and dying
> religious congregations of the Western Church.
> Sister Scholastica and Father Faricy show us how to
> shift the basis of our attempts at renewal from the
> interminably revolving cycle of discussion and from
> the forests of paper in which we feebly hope to the
> original source of each of our congregations – the
> breath of the Holy Spirit, breathing where it will.
> Let us lift our faces to that wind, to that gale which
> alone can sweep us into the future he is designing."
> LUCY ROONEY, S.N.D. DE N.

*"This work is full of hope and realistic optimism held out to
modern religious and to any Christian pondering the future
of a dedicated life in a religious community."* FROM THE
FOREWORD BY GEORGE MALONEY

ISBN 1-878718-02-9   80 pp. $6.95

Another Fine Book from Resurrection Press

A PATH TO HOPE
for Parents of Aborted Children and Those Who Minister to Them

John J. Dillon
Foreword by James P. Lisante

The pain and distress of Post-Abortion Syndrome are gradually and alarmingly coming to light as counselors see more and more victims of P.A.S. who cry out for healing. Drawing on his own considerable experience with parents of aborted children, Fr. Dillon succinctly describes the spiritual and psychological aftermath of abortion and offers solid guidelines and compassionate advice to those who counsel, minister to or journey with them. The issue of excommunication is discussed, and guidelines for a Healing Service are included.

"Should be a required textbook for anyone who wants to be involved in post-abortion ministry." VICKI THORN, FOUNDER
PROJECT RACHEL

"A gift for all who seek to be healers and reconcilers...a special grace for the hurting seeking the freedom of God's boundless love." FR. JAMES P. LISANTE, DIRECTOR
OFFICE OF FAMILY MINISTRY
DIOCESE OF ROCKVILLE CENTRE

"John Dillon understands the pain of aborted parents and gets right to where they are hurting. This is a wonderful how-to book." SUSAN KLESZEWSKI, M.S.W., L.C.S.W.
PSYCHOTHERAPIST

Fr. John J. Dillon is a spokesperson for Project Rachel in the Diocese of Rockville Centre, NY, and has lectured extensively throughout the country on the issue of post-abortion ministry.

ISBN 1-878718-00-2   80 pp. $5.95

Exclusively from Resurrection Press!
Spirit-Life Audiocassettes by Fr. Robert Lauder

PRAYING ON YOUR FEET
A Contemporary Spirituality for
Active Christians

Fr. Robert Lauder

Ever feel guilty about being too busy to pray? Here is the personal witness of a busy priest who struggled with this question until he realized that all Christian action is prayer and all prayer is a form of Christian action. Fr. Lauder assures us that spirituality in today's world can be achieved on our feet as well as on our knees.

SLC89-101   45 min. $6.95

HAIL VIRGIN MOTHER!
A Tribute to Mary

Fr. Robert Lauder

In his second tape for the Spirit-Life Collection, Father Robert Lauder focuses on Mary as the first believer and disciple and as the prime communicator of faith and faithfulness. He paints a true and full picture of the Virgin Mother for our greater appreciation of the mystery and meaning of the motherhood of God.

"Mary has a magnificent role in the history of salvation and in your life and my life, and therefore we should have a deep relationship with her." Listening to this tape will help you relate to Mary in a balanced and meaningful way.

SLC90-104   60 min. $6.95

RVC LITURGICAL SERIES

Whether you are actively involved in liturgical ministry, or simply wish better to understand the whys and wherefores of our Catholic Christian celebration, the RVC Liturgical Series will help you.

No. 1 OUR LITURGY
Your Guide to the Basics

Describes and discusses the nature and varieties of Liturgical Ministry, and clearly explains Liturgical Objects and The of Mass.

ISBN 0-9623410-1-0   64 pp. $4.25

No. 2 THE GREATEST SEASONS
Your Guide to Celebrating

Valuable insights for parish liturgy planning and to deepen personal liturgical celebration of the special times of the Church year.

ISBN 0-9623410-4-5   48 pp. $3.95

No. 3 THE LITURGY OF THE HOURS
Your Guide to Prayer

Explains the spiritual and liturgical background and the structure of the Divine Office, introduces you to the Psalms, and provides suggestions for parish implementation.

ISBN 0-9623410-7-X   48 pp. $3.95

No. 4 THE LECTOR'S MINISTRY
Your Guide to Proclaiming the Word

Provides invaluable basic practical advice on expressive reading and logistics, and also encourages and inspires lectors to adopt a prophetic spirituality which will both nourish them personally and empower them to be eleoquent witnesses of God's Word.

ISBN 0-9623410-4-5   48 pp. $3.95

"Commendable books for popular distribution." PASTORAL MUSIC

Another Fine Book from Resurrection Press

FROM THE WEAVER'S LOOM
Reflections on the Sundays and Feasts

Donald Hanson

A sought-after priest and preacher offers sensitive and spiritual reflections for each Sunday of the year and some special feasts and holydays. Each reflection weaves together threads of various textures and hues: an understanding of the scripture passage; the rhythm and tone of each Sunday and feast; the cores of people's struggles, hopes and dreams. You will not only find them a thought-provoking source for private meditation – you will also be uplifted by Fr. Hanson's gift for transforming a vital pastoral function into a beautiful work of art.

"These meditative reflections are an entree into the liturgical year, designed to help, inspire and encourage Christians who celebrate God's Word in the Sunday assembly. Don Hanson offers a rich festal fare to whet the palate before the liturgical banquet or to prolong the celebration. However they are enjoyed, they will provide sustenance for the Christian spirit."
JOHN ALLYN MELLOH, SM, UNIVERSITY OF NOTRE DAME

"This book sets forth the mysteries of faith in a compelling and artistic fashion. It should be helpful to all homilists."
REV. RONALD F. KRISMAN, EXECUTIVE DIRECTOR
SECRETARIAT FOR THE LITURGY

Fr. Donald Hanson has been Liturgy Coordinator, Bishop's Master of Ceremonies and Vice Chancellor for the Diocese of Rockville Centre, NY. He is now pastor of St. Joseph's in Babylon, NY.

ISBN 1-87818-01-0   160 pp. $7.95

Another Fine Book from Resurrection Press

GIVE THEM SHELTER
Responding to Hunger and Homelessness

Michael Moran

Thanks to over 1,200 volunteers of all faiths and races, The INN has successfully addressed the needs of the hungry and homeless on Long Island. INN Director Mike Moran shares this true story with wisdom, humor and compassion. You will be amazed and inspired by the birth and growth of The INN's soup kitchens and emergency shelters; the interfaith network of volunteers, food sources and donations maintaining The INN; the breakdown of the underlying causes of hunger and homelessness.

"The tale of The INN is a simple one indeed. It is a tale of simple decencies in a world where people still matter...It's a reminder that one man can make a difference and goodness, like evil, will spread outward in ever widening concentric circles.

Michael Moran's story, the tale of The INN, will change the world of those who read it and choose not to look away." ROBERT M. HAYES, FOUNDER
NATIONAL COALITION FOR THE HOMELESS

ISBN 0-9623410-6-1   120 pp. $5.95

Other Titles Available from Resurrection Press

His Healing Touch *Michael Buckley* $7.95
A Celebration of Life *Anthony Padovano* $7.95
Miracle in the Marketplace *Henry Libersat* $5.95
Transformed by Love *Margaret Magdalen, CSMV* $5.95
Behold the Man *Judy Marley, SFO* $3.50
I Shall Be Raised Up $2.25

Our Spirit-Life Audiocassette Collection

Celebrating the Vision of Vatican II *Michael Himes* $6.95
Annulment: Healing-Hope-New Life *Thomas Molloy* $6.95
Divided Loyalties *Anthony Padovano* $6.95

Resurrection Press books and cassettes are available in your local religious bookstore. In case of difficulty, or if you wish to be on our mailing list free of charge for our up-to-date announcements, please write or phone:

Resurrection Press
P.O. Box 248
Williston Park, NY 11596
(516) 742-5686

When pre-paying your order, please enclose $1.50 for the first item and 50¢ for each additional item. Maximum $4.00.